T0355016

Peripheral Vision

Cat Schmidt

Order this book online at www.trafford.com
or email orders@trafford.com

Most Trafford titles are also available at major online book retailers.

Printed in the United States of America.

ISBN: 978-1-4269-6195-3(sc)

Trafford rev. 06/13/2011

www.trafford.com

North America & international
toll-free: 1 888 232 4444 (USA & Canada)
phone: 250 383 6864 • fax: 812 355 4082

Contents

Introduction

My name is Cat Schmidt and I live near Houston, Texas. Writing this book has been a challenge as I work full time. I am also the mother of four wonderful children who are dealing with the joys and responsibilities of adulthood, marriage and parenting. I am happily remarried, well most of the time. How many couples actually experience marital bliss? Just when you think you have your life planned perfectly along comes that special person who turns your world upside down. When I think of how my second husband came into my world I have to admit that he really did turn things upside down. I soon realized my shining star was more like an asteroid. (Just kidding of course). Sometimes my husband is my shining star, and really lights up my world. Let's face it; all marriages have their dark, cloudy days, but true love will prevail. Regardless, our marriage has survived nearly twenty years. I was born and raised in this sultry city of the deep south and currently live in the suburbs. In Houston it's hard to tell where the city ends and the suburbs begin but I guess when you see the prostitutes standing at the corner, the drug dealers waving you down, or the smell of industry you know you are getting close to the city. Despite that I am still a Texan at heart. One thing that really bothers me though is the stigma that many people have of Texas, that we are still part of the Wild West and that everyone wears cowboy hats while they drive their colossal gas sucking pick up trucks on one of those lonely winding, country roads occasionally spitting their chewed tobacco out the window. That just isn't a true portrayal of my state. God forbid there are no cowgirl hats sitting atop my closet shelf and when I do wear jeans it is with a sheik T shirt. There are no tumbleweeds blowing across our well manicured lawn and even though I may have that Texas drawl when I speak, I am quite urbanized. So if you ever visit our lovely state, you may be surprised. Of course there may be a few places that are stuck in the past such as the small towns that sprinkle the landscape between the big cities. But if you stay on the interstate you will be completely oblivious to their existence. Now if you ever decide to visit my town and you saw me in line at the grocery store I wouldn't stand out. I would look pretty much like any of the middle-aged ladies in line going through my coupons before I got to the check out. The thing that makes me different is while most people in line at the grocery store are checking off their grocery list, chatting on their cell phones or thinking about their confused lives, I would be thinking of ways to change things. We definitely need change but our overpaid, vacationing lawmakers and government officials are lagging behind. When new legislation is presented they bicker back and forth, toiling over every word and when they can't make a decision they call for recess and go play golf or do whatever makes them happy as long as it doesn't involve that four letter word, work. The politicians also spend too much time hanging out with the lobbyists. Their political stamina goes right down the drain as they make deals behind closed doors with those one-sided lobbyists. We all know lobbyist represent special interests, big companies and the like. What they do not represent is you or me. I believe they do not belong in our places of government for that reason. Of course my life is much simpler. I don't have any lobbyist dangling cash on a stick in front of me, so I can make my own decisions, of course on a much smaller scale. And that is my goal, to suggest ways to make our lives a little better in this great country. For instance let's go back to the grocery store; it is always a struggle for the clerk to find my brand of cigarettes. I guess with so many cigarette brands it is confusing for the clerk to find my brand, especially if they don't smoke. There are so many choices, regular or light cigarettes, ultra light, menthol and so on. So I would devise a numbered chart to locate my brand. The numbered chart would correspond to a numbered bin where the cigarette packs are kept. The chart would be available at every check out counter and I would simply say I need a pack of number seventeen. This is my quest, to simplify life so we can enjoy it more. I've had a pretty good life so far so maybe it's time to give back. I guess I feel anxious about all the things in our society that I feel I have no control over. Our messed up society is getting more messed up everyday, and I do not want to tolerate it any longer. If we (the human race), do not make some drastic changes in our behavior towards each other and our planet, I believe it is just a matter of time before God decides to flush the overflowing toilet bowl of humanity so to speak. God must have a lot of patience because we humans continually screw things up, we can't get along with each other and we have basically ruined our beautiful planet. I on the other hand, am running out of patience. There's too much of our hard earned money going into that black hole called government, and not enough getting done for the common people or to save the planet by conserving our resources. So that's why I decided to write a book, to address the issues that really bug me. Nowadays anyone can write a book, so why can't I? I have this overwhelming feeling that if I did not attempt this, I would have a space in my life that was unaccounted for. Sort of like pressing the delete button on your computer accidentally. I don't want to be in a situation in my later life saying, "I had a chance to say something, but I remained quite". So here is the product of all my anxieties and ideas. Now let me put all the seriousness aside for a moment and share a secret. I have this crazy dream of appearing on one of those afternoon talk shows one day to promote my book. I imagine that after I make my awkward entrance and am seated, I cross my legs, then pull out my cigarette case and light one up. It would be so cool if I really could smoke during my few minutes of fame, like they did in the old days. But I know the TV stations probably don't allow smoking in the studios anymore. I still have images of all those past celebrities on various TV talk shows where they are seated, with their legs crossed, and amidst their discussions they light up a cigarette. They looked so cool and glamorous. Well I might be a dreamer but I am also a realist. My goal is to provide a whimsical analogy of today's world in this literary cocktail of mine and perhaps leave a small imprint on someone's mind. You know, or you may not know, that life is short. I feel it is important to do something you enjoy in life, as long as it's legal and not too weird. If anyone tries to prevent you from doing what you enjoy, consider them your enemy and stray far from that person because life is the sum of everything we do and don't do in this world. I believe it is better to have tried and not succeeded, than never have attempted to achieve one's goals. I know I should have done this a long time ago, but there's no time like the fucking present. No offense intended but sometimes you need a little eye opener if you want to get your point across which is my whole objective. One more thing, I have written many chapters which represent my ideas and concerns, but I have also strayed a little and written about some of my personal experiences. I just thought it would be a good idea to break the monotony from time to time. Besides, life should be filled with little surprises.

Driving Me Crazy

We spend more time than we probably realize behind the wheel. I believe most people are good, responsible drivers and deserve the privilege of driving but what about the rest of the driving population? I can't even drive out of my subdivision without using the word "dumb ass", of course referring to other drivers that frustrate me when I just want to get where I'm going. Aside from bad drivers there are other issues that need to be addressed which could change who can drive. Who should be able to drive and what criteria should a driver have to meet before that get behind the wheel? That is what I will address in these next chapters. Our roadways are getting too congested and we are burning more and more fossil fuels, it's almost as though no one is paying attention to this ongoing problem. So maybe it's time to make some changes across the board.

On the Road Again

First of all I am not writing about "Willie Nelson's" music in this chapter. I respect the man and his talent, but I am writing about the challenges of driving in a big city. If you have ever visited Houston, Texas and had the experience of driving on our freeways then you may understand how congested the traffic is. If you live in or around Houston you cannot survive without wheels. The city is very spread out and continues to sprawl outward and consume more and more real estate. As a consequence, there is construction going on everywhere. This relates to detours, freeway closings, and having to maneuver around all the construction sites, which look more like destruction sites. What we really need is a futuristic train or rail system that transports people to their destination in a quick and comfortable manner. We do have a light rail system that caters to the downtown area however most of the population lives in the suburbs, so it isn't a benefit to most of us. The city politicians need to get off their lazy asses and do something quick. Unfortunately I don't see the light at the end of the tunnel. By the time the city officials get it approved I will be dust in the wind. So we Houstonians are stuck with our current mass transit system which basically sucks. It consists of buses and more buses. These are really big buses that move slowly and block lanes when they are picking up passengers. I have had a few occasions to ride the bus, such as when I got picked for jury duty and had to report to the downtown courthouse. No one in their right mind would want to drive to downtown Houston. The parking is expensive and hard to find. If you're selected for jury duty, the courts pay for your bus fare, so it makes sense to go by bus. The first thing I noticed about the buses is how cold and uncomfortable they are. I guess it's good that they're air conditioned but as you step onto the bus the cold air hits you, sort of like a burst of air from an artic cold front. It could be 100 degrees outside, which in Houston is very possible in the months of July, August and September, but it will be cold on the bus. And it must have some effect on the passengers, who seem as cold as the air. If one can tolerate the cold air and the hard plastic seats for a short time they can get downtown much faster on the bus. That's because the buses can travel on the HOV lanes that are reserved for multi passenger vehicles. The other alternative to get around Houston is to drive on the toll roads. This is sort of like the Houston Audubon as everyone drives as fast as they can, passing the speed limit signs with total disregard. I believe they drive this way because they have to pay to drive on the toll roads and they want to get their money's worth. So unless you're a race car driver or you ride the bus your other option is to drive on the congested freeways and byways to get around town. But I have some ideas to make driving a little more tolerable by narrowing down the driving population. It would take years and years to construct the mega freeways or to build the futuristic rail system, so I think it's time to downsize the number of vehicles on the road. Let's face it, not everybody that drives should be allowed to, so let's see who we can eliminate so to speak. And this doesn't just apply to Houston, I'm thinking of any city in America. Regardless of where the wheels hit the pavement we need to make changes.

Pop Wrecked the Car

My husband's grandfather was often referred to as "Pop". I thought the name was cute, and I also referred to him as Pop in the short time I knew him. He was an amusing old gentleman, who was happy to sip on a beer, smoke a cigarette and watch TV. He was definitely my kind of guy. The problem was that he lived alone in his last years and had the occasional urge to drive to the store, or wherever it was he wanted to go. The other problem was that he was not always in his right mind as he would often forget things, including how to drive. While he was in his eighties, on a bright sunny Florida day, he decided to go for a drive, and upon exiting his neighborhood onto the main street, forgot to check for any traffic coming his way, pulled out onto the main street and caused an accident. Fortunately no one was hurt and everyone soon realized he should not have been driving. But what gets me is how he was able to keep his drivers license in the first place. And why did he have to get involved in an accident before everyone realized he should not be driving? He was already what I consider to be old when I met him, of course someone who is seventy five may not think eighty is too old to be driving, but let's get real, eighty is old. There had been many clues surfacing over the years which indicated he was loosing his facilities so to speak. One day my husband's father found him wandering down the street, oblivious to where he was. He also had a habit of allowing people from his neighborhood to come into his home, rather they were invited or not. Consequently many of his possessions started disappearing. But all this should have been a warning sign to his family, friends and doctor. I might be sinking my own ship, but I feel the legal driving age should not exceed 65 without a screening process in place. After 65 our elders could receive a special permit to drive which would be good for one or two years. I am just suggesting a way to monitor these drivers who could cause injury to themselves or someone else. If they are able to pass a health exam, their doctor would sign off for them to be able to drive. Without their doctor's approval, their driving days would be over, or limited. Because I think some of the older generation may be able to drive in certain conditions, such as daytime only, and they could receive a restricted permit to drive. This type of permit is already in use in Texas. Let's face it, if you are lucky and make it to old age, you might also be lucky enough to have family or friends to drive you where you need to go, like the grocery store, the bank, the golf course, the church or wherever. If you are not lucky enough to have family or friends to drive you, then there should be some transportation system in place that could pick you up. At some point you must admit to yourself when that time arrives and you are no longer able to drive. Then you can just relax and enjoy the precious time you have left. I'm sure an old person doesn't get up in the morning and suddenly realize they are not able to drive. But as one reaches those golden years their senses start to deteriorate and at some point they need to accept the fact that they shouldn't drive. By restricting the driving age to sixty five and then requiring medical consent for every couple of years or so after sixty five; one could monitor which of our elders shouldn't be driving. Right now in Texas the Department of Public Safety will automatically renew your driver's license on-line or by mail so there is no process in place to screen a person's medical or mental health. If a new law imposed such screenings after the age of sixty five many lives could be saved. Imagine an elderly person makes to age seventy only to be killed or permanently injured in an auto accident they caused. Not to mention the fate of the other driver. It's not fair, especially if it's your parent or grandparent. They should be home making cookies, working in the garden or doing whatever they enjoy during those golden years. And their children, grandchildren, family members, friends or community should ensure they have a way to be transported when there is a need. After all I think they deserve the special treatment.

Change the Legal Driving Age

Simply put, the legal driving age should be changed to eighteen years old. Even though it may only be a small sector of the population, eliminating the age group of sixteen and seventeen year old drivers could help remove some of the traffic congestion, especially in the morning hours when all the children are driving to school. And I emphasize the word "children" because they are children. It's not the parent's fault that they let their children drive, but rather peer pressure because if other kids get to drive, it's only expected that their kid will want to drive. So I say let the government intercede by changing the law, and the parents will finally be able to breathe a sigh of relief. Not only will this have a small impact on the traffic, but how do you think these kids afford their cars? Some of them get part-time jobs. If they don't have a car, they don't need a job, and guess what, now more jobs are available for the rest of the population. Hey, I'm not anti-youth. I was sixteen when I started driving and most of the time I was a responsible driver. Notice I said most of the time. My driving days started innocently enough, driving back and forth to school with a few of my friends and younger brother in tow. Call it fate or whatever, but just as soon as I started driving they lowered the legal age to buy alcohol from twenty one to eighteen in Texas. Of course that was back in the 1970's. How convenient as I had the freedom to drive and even though I was only sixteen or seventeen years old at the time; I could easily pass for eighteen years old at the corner store that sold alcoholic beverages. This newly found freedom eventually led to drinking and driving. So there went my innocence right out the car window along with my cigarette butts as I cruised around. Back in the seventies I remember driving and drinking a beer while a cop was parked right next to me at a red stoplight. I didn't even have a seat belt on because the seat belt law had not gone into effect. The cop looked at me, I looked at him raising my can of beer as a friendly gesture, the light turned green and we both went our separate ways. That memory really blows my mind today. If that had happened today I would be going to jail. But you have to wonder, how many teenage drivers have died or been seriously injured due to careless driving? I shutter at the thought. You see where I'm going with this? I just don't think teenagers are mature enough to drive. Their brains are still forming until they are eighteen, nineteen or twenty something, so they're just not ready to be in control of an automobile. I believe if the law is changed everyone will be happy, except the insurance companies because they like to insure high risk individuals. So simply stated, if you're not old enough to vote, or go to war, or pay taxes, or buy a lottery ticket you shouldn't be allowed to drive. Maybe while those teenagers are at home, they could watch little brother or mow the yard? What a concept. And if they can't find anything to do there's always homework. At the very least these soon to be drivers could save their allowance or babysitting money so that by the time they graduate from high school they could save enough money for a down payment on a car. This would teach them financial responsibility. And by the time they are eighteen years old they deserve the privilege to drive and be free spirits. Hopefully they will drive to and from college and become well educated, responsible adults who will make our society a better place. But wherever they choose to drive when they're eighteen they will have earned that privilege.

Seeing Double

There are many weekend nights that my husband and I have enjoyed listening to music and having a few drinks as we try to forget about the workweek. I usually make the run to the local liquor store for my husband as he prefers liquor while I like to enjoy a couple of cold ones. I'm sure millions of Americans do the same but let it be known that I do not condone drinking and driving. I have to plead

"Cheers"

guilty along with those millions of Americans who have done it, drinking and driving that is, but that doesn't make it right. While serving alcohol is a very profitable business there is very little responsibility for business owners who reap the rewards of serving alcohol and send the drunk merrily on their way without a second thought. I'm surprised that the police don't sit outside nightclubs waiting to pounce on the drunken party goers who have no choice but to leave at 2:00 am because that's when most of the clubs and bars close. This act alone could save many lives by recognizing and restraining the drunk driver before they have a chance to drive off. However, the police may feel it is not their responsibility. It is up to each individual to be responsible for their actions, and thus the police do not interfere until there is a consequence. Well, I have a couple of ideas to remedy the situation. First of all why not have breakfast bars at nightclubs? This could encourage the guests to have a cup of Joe and something to eat before they leave the nightclub. The nightclubs or bars could offer breakfast for their guests say from 12:00am till whenever they close. The breakfast bar could be complimentary or the establishment could charge a small price for some coffee and scrambled eggs. It might help "undue" some of the damage from drinking all night. My second suggestion is to have "valet" parking only for any establishment that serves alcohol. I know this is a radical solution but drinking and driving just isn't cool. When a guest appears to be too intoxicated to drive, they simply wouldn't get their car. I remember back in the good old days, my husband and I went to a nightclub one night. We had fun drinking and dancing, and my husband drove us home. I thought my husband's driving was fine. When we arrived home, he proceeded to get out of the truck, took a few steps to the curb side, laid down on the grass and was out like a light. I think he was overtired but the alcohol enhanced his fatigue to the point that he couldn't go any further. I tried to get him up and finally after much persuasion he got up, slowly climbed the stairs to our apartment and passed out again for the night. I wondered after the fact how he had managed to drive home. He must have been on auto-pilot or perhaps his guardian angel was watching over him.

With mandatory valet parking, the nightclubs could be in control of who drives and who doesn't drive. I think this is a great idea that could save lives. During the hours that alcohol is served one would arrive at the establishment and have their vehicle parked by the valet. If the establishment is a restaurant they would receive a stamp on their hand or some way to identify that they are valet parked. This would also include any guests in their party. Once inside the establishment they could be served alcohol only if they have the recognizable stamp or other identification that they are valet parked. Of course if someone is dropped off by a cab or other means, the valet personnel could stamp their hand to allow them to drink alcohol. This may seem an extreme measure but it is really a small price to pay for one's safety. When one leaves the establishment to retrieve their vehicle they must be sober enough to drive. Obviously anyone who presents signs of being intoxicated such as staggering, slurred speech or loud and belligerent behavior would not receive their vehicle. In the event someone is intoxicated the establishment could offer to call a cab. If the intoxicated person refuses a cab and demands their car, the police could be called to remedy the situation. This act alone could prevent an accident or at the very least that person would not have to worry about getting in trouble with the law. Right now the laws are not proactive, but rather reactive, because they do not try to prevent drinking and driving. My idea is to think of ways to prevent the act, before it happens. The laws need to be set forth and made understandable to everyone. Right now the offenders are tried on a case by case basis. One could spend a small fortune paying all the legal fines and court expenses if they are caught driving and drinking, or under the influence of alcohol. Some offenders can drive if they have a device in their vehicle that detects alcohol on their breath. But all that is defeating the basis of the problem. I say let's make the laws proactive to prevent drinking and driving and start saving lives. Now some may think the valet parking idea would be difficult for restaurants to enforce, but I don't think it would be that hard. The restaurants would simply section off a part of the parking lot and those who wished to consume alcohol would drive to that section.

Those who did not wish to consume alcohol would park normally. The patrons that want to drink alcohol would have to present proof that they were valet parked. It's really that simple. As for nightclubs many of them already have valet parking as an option, they would just have to set up the whole parking lot as valet parking only. Of course the best solution is to drink at home. If you want to socialize and drink, get the neighbors together for a block party. If you want to go to a nightclub, either have a designated driver, or call a cab. A $50.00 cab ride is a small price to pay compared to thousands of dollars of legal expenses, or the price of someone losing their life. If you go out with friends and share the cost of the cab fare, it's really not that much. I also think it would be a good idea if liquor stores would resume the practice of delivering to their customer's homes. Let's face it, humans have been enjoying spirits for thousands of years, and will continue to do so. If you know someone who is not being responsible take matters into your own hands by refusing to ride with that person, or offering to drive them home. Of course if my idea was implemented nationwide we could monitor the problem drinkers before they drive off, perhaps some of them never reaching their destination.

Zoned Out

I'm sure both parents usually have to work in today's world, especially with the cost of living continually going up not to mention the cost of raising children. I know some of you parents out there won't like this chapter, but I'm thinking of the safety of your children. I suggest we change the public school hours to where the buses and parents are not taking their kids to school before 8:00 am or picking them up after 4:00 pm. The schools could be in session from 8:30 am to 3:30 pm. That's six and a half hours of teaching with one half hour for lunch if you do the math. This would allow the school related traffic to be clear when most of us are driving to work in the morning, or driving home from work in the afternoon. I don't know how they would do it, but believe me there is a way. Our children will have to face an eight hour work day when they become adults, so why not give them a break? This policy should go into effect for all public and private school zones as it is safer for everyone concerned. There should be a national law that no school zones can be enforced before say 7: 45 am or after 4:15 pm. Perhaps they could gradually add class hours to each school year, for example pre-school and kindergarten attend school half a day, but I have heard of all day classes for kindergarten. These are five year old children and they shouldn't have to attend school more than fours hours a day. They should be at home playing and discovering their world. I believe they're still young and should nap during the day. So with that in mind perhaps pre-school and kindergarten classes should only last four hours a day. Now first and second grade could attend five hours a day and third grade to twelfth grade could attend a full day. My daughter currently teaches 2nd grade. Their school hours are 8:05 A.M. to 3:05 P.M. That's a seven hour day. I think four to five hours of instructional learning with one hour of recreation, or other non-instructional setting would be sufficient. Remember children bring home homework on a daily basis. Imagine as a parent if you had to come home and do homework after a hard day of work? This would be overwhelming to say the least. Not to mention that many children are also involved in other activities such as sports, dance classes and so on. With a shorter school day one wouldn't have to worry about the school zones which usually go into effect at 7:00 am. Frustrated commuters wouldn't have to mingle with school buses on their way to or from work. This would be a win, win situation for everyone concerned because it would provide extra safety for our children and less traffic for the commuters. Our children would be more rested and thus more focused when they do go to school. If you read the chapter "Time to Focus on Education", I suggest removing all non-academic classes from our public schools. If this was done it would be easier to schedule a shorter school day thus allowing the school zones to start later in the morning and end earlier in the afternoon. As for the parents who work and provide transportation to or from school for their children, I believe a law should go into effect which would allow parents time off that reason. This law could allow parents to do so without penalty from their employer such as removing their full time status or eligibility for benefits. I like to make things easier for everyone concerned, from the pre-school tot to the parents who work hard to provide for their families and all those commuters who just want to get to work on time.

Driving in America

Houston is a very culturally diverse city. We are close to Mexico, thus Mexicans, legal and illegal, make up a huge part of our population. Oriental and Middle Eastern races also contribute to a large sector of the population. It's bad enough when you have to drive with all the idiots on the road who probably think you're an idiot as well, now add people who cannot read, speak or understand English to the mix, and you've got trouble. On numerous occasions I have witnessed foreigners who were at the local gas station and would approach the counter to pay for their goods. I noticed they didn't speak a word of English as the clerk would attempt to communicate with them the best they could. Then they would exit the store only to get into a vehicle and drive off. Now I don't have anything against immigration, as I'm sure my great, great grandparents came from some other country. And I don't mind being neighborly, however if you want to drive in our beautiful nation I believe you should be a legal citizen or have a legal drivers license from your country of origin. Anyone who is an immigrant should have to present their driver's license to the proper authorities before they get to drive on our roads. They should also be given a translation of our traffic signs and laws before they get to drive. This would insure they understand the traffic signs and the basic traffic laws which may vary some from their country of origin. Imagine if you were driving to work one morning, and all the traffic signs were written in Chinese! (I hope this is not a premonition). You would probably be confused and perhaps a little panicked. No doubt this is how our immigrant population feels when they see the traffic signs written in English. What happens if they get the "Yield" and "Stop" signs mixed up? In addition these immigrant drivers must also provide proof of liability insurance as it is required by law. If I decided to visit a foreign country I would study the language first. I may not master the language, but at least I would try to learn the basics. I see so many of our immigrants who don't even try to learn English. And basically they don't have to. Society, as I know it, seems to cater to these non English speaking individuals. I have seen billboards written in Spanish, and if you go the grocery store nowadays, the products are labeled in English and Spanish. Convenience is one thing, but when you have people driving around who can't read the traffic signs it is more than an inconvenience, it is a formula for disaster. There is also a huge problem in Texas of illegal immigrants who drive without a license. I believe there is just not enough police to prevent this from happening and the illegal immigrants know this and take advantage of our system. So I suggest that the police start setting up blockades and checking all vehicles for driver's license, insurance and registration. The blockades could be set up at random locations and times and could check say fifty vehicles at a time. If they did this on a regular basis the number of offenders caught would probably be significant. Some may feel the blockades are too "Gestapo like", but when there are not enough police to enforce the driving population this method could be very effective. Once the offenders are caught there could be a problem of getting them to show up in court. If they are illegal immigrants do you think they will show up in court? Hell no. So they would need to be detained until their court date arrives and if they do not have papers to be here legally, it is "adios amigos", and back to whatever country they came from. I'm sure these illegal immigrants who drive illegally don't have the liability insurance required either. So when they cause an accident guess who's going to pay for the damages? The insured driver, and as a result the cost of insurance continues to go up. It's rather unfortunate that in Houston our so called "mass transit" system really sucks. And because Houston is so spread out the mass transit system doesn't reach all areas of town. This makes it almost a necessity to drive, but despite that if one is an illegal immigrant they shouldn't be here in the first place, much less should they be driving around, carelessly and uninsured. So until that fateful day arrives when traffic signs are multilingual, and this could happen sooner than you think, our foreign population should be able to read English enough to understand the traffic signs and have a basic understanding of the driving laws. I guess the other alternative would be to change the traffic signs to "symbols" if you will. I believe this is the way to go but imagine the cost involved to change out all the signs. So we need to make changes now or things could get progressively worse. All visitors from other countries should provide a legal driver's license from the country of origin along with proof of liability insurance. If their country does not require liability insurance they should be required to purchase a policy. Perhaps a short term policy could be made available to purchase for tourists and visitors. The laws need to be more stringent and the lawmakers must think of more creative ways to enforce the laws. It is only fair to those who drive responsibly and abide by the laws.

Who's Liable?

I don't know about other cities, but in Houston, Texas there are probably thousands of uninsured drivers. As I mentioned before there are many illegal immigrants who drive without a license or liability insurance. Even though it is the law in Texas to have liability insurance many drive with total disregard of the law. I think it is a good law because in the event that you cause an accident, the liability insurance would help pay for damages to the other person's vehicle and perhaps medical expenses if they are injured. One pays their premium and they are issued an insurance card which usually goes in the glove box of their vehicle. My insurance company issues a new card every six months. But with millions of people living in the Houston area it would be impossible to know who is insured and who is not. Now I hate being judgmental but when I see one of those old clunker cars on the road, I sometimes assume the party driving that car is uninsured. When I see tape on any part of a vehicle or a tail pipe that is barely hanging on, I get that feeling. That feeling tells me not to get to close to that vehicle because the driver probably couldn't afford insurance. Now liability insurance is not that expensive however many drive under the insurance radar because you're only required to show proof of insurance if you are stopped by the police or when it's time to renew your registration or get your vehicle inspected which is a state law. I have also had to show proof of insurance when renewing my driver's license unless I do so by mail or on-line. That is one of the loopholes in the system, if you get your license renewed in person you have to show proof of insurance, but not if you renew on-line or by mail. Herein lie's the problem. Many people get the required insurance when they need it for renewing their license or registration. Then they make one or two monthly payments and let the policy lapse. But now they have the proof of insurance card they need because the stupid insurance companies issue the card up front for a period of six months to a year as soon as they get the first payment. And most people prefer to pay for the insurance monthly as opposed to paying for six months or a year up front because it is easier on their budget. It makes me really mad because people take advantage of the system while other people abide by the rules. If you are involved in an accident with someone who is uninsured you most likely have to file an insurance claim with your own insurance company to cover the expenses. Then you may notice a price increase when your policy renews. Or the insurance company may cancel your policy. In other words you get punished because the piece of shit that caused the accident didn't have insurance. This also relates to "hit and run" accidents. The person causing the accident leaves the scene to avoid prosecution. My mother in law was a victim of this type of accident. Thankfully she was not injured. I'm sure many of these uninsured feel they cannot afford the insurance. Well, guess what, they shouldn't be driving! Then there are those who probably could afford the insurance, but they just want to beat the system. And I would like to beat them, with a big stick. So I think I have the solution, and I don't mean the big stick I just referred to. In the state of Texas one must have their vehicle registered once a year. You may also have to have your vehicle inspected once a year, depending on the county you live in. Once you receive the new registration or inspection you are issued a decal to be displayed on the driver's side of the windshield. Here's my idea, what if there was an adhesive plastic holder for the registration, inspection and the proof of insurance. Notice I said "proof of insurance"? I feel the proof of liability insurance should be displayed on the windshield so it would be in plain view. If the proof of insurance is in the glove box it is hidden away. But if it was displayed on the windshield it would be in plain sight for the police to see. This is how to solve the problem of people cheating the system. The insurance companies could give people an option of paying for the insurance quarterly, semi annually or annually and the paper would show the coverage dates in big numbers so the police could tell if the insurance coverage had expired. In other words if I paid my insurance premium three months in advance that date would be reflected on the paper I place inside my windshield. I would replace the paper with the renewal proof of insurance each time I made a payment. The insurance companies would probably stop offering monthly premiums because it would be ridiculous to issue new paperwork on a monthly basis, but most people could pay quarterly if needed. For people who pay for collision insurance also, which protects them and their vehicle; perhaps the premiums could be billed monthly. I currently pay my premiums monthly for both liability and collision. If my insurance company could break down the cost I could pay the liability premiums quarterly and the collision premiums monthly. It would just take a little budgeting but people could get used to it. Now I'm sure there would be dishonest people who would try to counterfeit the proof of insurance but that's just human nature. Perhaps the insurance paperwork could provide a toll free phone number for law officials to call if they needed to verify coverage. Another way to prevent counterfeiting the paperwork would be a code for the type of vehicle that is insured. For instance let's say I drive a shiny black Ford F-150 truck. My proof of insurance could show "Black" for the color of vehicle I drive. It would be easy for a police officer to match the color of the vehicle to the proof of insurance paperwork. Let's say someone stole the insurance paperwork from the inside of my windshield and put it on their red pickup truck, the description would not match their vehicle. Or the insurance companies could reference part of the VIN number on the proof of insurance. What a genius idea. You know the real epitome of this ordeal is that people are so pitiful. These lazy and weak minded individuals steal and cheat their way through the system. So now it's time for the rest of us to take control and hold these people accountable. You know, it's not that hard to come up with these solutions. It just takes a common sense approach and some guts to change the system. Remember the "plastic pocket" that I referred to earlier which adheres to the inside of the windshield? I really like this idea because the documents are currently printed on stickers and its a little tricky putting them on. And if you ever have to replace your windshield, the stickers have to be peeled off, and get all wrinkled or torn. With the plastic pockets you just take the plastic pocket off the old windshield if you have to have it replaced and put it on the new windshield. I guess if the "windshield pockets" really did catch on they could be mass produced and someone enterprising out there could make a lot of money. Now back to business, if you are in an accident with someone who is uninsured you have very little recourse. You could take that person to court, but good luck, they probably wouldn't show up. If these dishonest people drive without the required insurance they are not going to wake up the next day and start being responsible, it is just not in their character. This is why we must make changes. My ideas are not complicated or costly, but rather an easy solution to an everyday problem which could give us all a little peace of mind the next time we drive. Now if I can come up with a solution why can't the insurance companies do the same? Well I guess they're just too busy counting all that money and figuring out how much to raise our premiums.

Planes and Automobiles

I grew up in the seventies when life was simpler. Back then gasoline was cheap and one could drive around for hours without really going anywhere. I was fortunate that my father was able to help me get my first car. No he didn't buy it for me but rather he knew someone who was selling their car and arranged for me to buy it. I worked part time so I could afford the low monthly payments. I can remember driving to school with my classmates and sometimes my younger brother who would tag along. It was a wonderful feeling because I was in control. Sometimes I would drive nowhere, meaning I would just drive down any road for the sake of driving. I had the windows rolled down and my hair blew in the wind while my radio played the songs of the day. When I was in my car no one could bother me because I was a free spirit. It was only when I reached my destination that I had to be accountable for my whereabouts. Now I had always dreamed of flying but I never had an opportunity to fly on an airplane until I was thirty four years old. As a young girl I watched movies of famous stars flying to Paris, New York and other worldly places, but I never thought that it would happen to me. Back in the seventies mostly wealthy people or businessmen flew as it was more expensive to travel by air. Now you may have noticed I said "businessmen" and there is a reason for that. Most women were at home taking care of their families in the seventies. We were at the verge of women's liberation but most of the women I knew stayed home. Now let me fast forward for a moment, I left off driving my car as a carefree teenager. After that many years passed and I met my soon to be second husband. We lived together for a short time and became engaged. Then one day my fiancé announced he was going to Florida to visit his father and he had purchased an airline ticket. He proceeded to ask me to visit him there on the weekend as I had to work during the week so I couldn't accompany him for the entire visit. My simple mind started to calculate the distance between Texas and Florida and snapshots of my Hyundai car appeared in my brain. I knew my car got pretty good gas mileage but it wasn't a fast car by any means. How was I going to drive to Florida on Friday and be back at work on Monday? Then my fiancé announced, "You will have to fly to Florida". Oh, I understood, I was going to be a jetsetter. After being on this earth for thirty four years I was finally going to experience flight, it was all very exciting. And it did turn out to be an exciting weekend that I will never forget. That same month I took my first airplane ride we got married, which was a grand finale to that wonderful month. It's funny how life changes so quickly. Now let me fast forward again. After my new husband and I were married for several years he announced we were going to visit his father in Florida again. So we decided to fly. This would be my second time to take flight. Little did I know what was going to happen on that fateful day as our vacation started and we drove to the airport with the bright morning sun shining on our smiling, naïve faces. We arrived at the airport and boarded the plane. The plane took off as we made small talk and discussed our vacation plans. It happened about mid flight as I heard those engine noises you don't want to hear. I glanced out the window from time to time to see the fluffy clouds and occasional patches of blue water in the Gulf of Mexico. We were suspended above the earth by thirty thousand feet or so and the airplane hit some very heavy turbulence and dropped very suddenly. I felt like I was on a wicked elevator ride where the floor had dropped out. We must have dropped what seemed several thousand feet or maybe several hundred feet and I screamed out loud. After I screamed out loud I looked at my husband who was obviously embarrassed and told me to be quite. I didn't understand how he could be so calm, but I subdued my panic as I tried to understand what had just happened. But before I could gather my composure that same turbulence that caused the plane drop several thousand feet or several hundred feet caused the plane to rise. The sudden ascent made me feel like we were going to leave the earth and rocket into space. This time almost everybody aboard screamed, except my husband of course who just look surprised. As the plane maneuvered through the turbulence I could hear the high pitch sounds of the engines again and wondered if we were going to make it. I know I consciously looked at the flight crew and they didn't look too confident which made me even more nervous. I felt my life flash in front of me as I nervously grabbed my husband and proceeded to ask "what the hell was that?" My husband explained that we had probably hit an air pocket which had caused the plane to drop and rise again. Well, that was it, that's all I needed to know as I decided I never wanted to experience it again. I told my husband at that point that I was going to kiss the ground if we ever made it to our destination. Of course the plane did finally land and I started thinking about the vow I had made to kiss the ground. After we landed I was so relieved to feel the ground under my feet that I allowed my husband and his father to walk ahead of me as I searched for my cigarette lighter. I really needed a cigarette. As we approached an inconspicuous part of the airport I noticed a pole and there were not too many people around so I proceeded to kiss the pole. I guess I rationalized I would look like an idiot if I bent down to kiss the ground so I compromised for the sake of my husband and his father and proceeded to kiss the pole instead. My husband didn't appreciate my compromise and yelled at me to "stop that". That day I vowed to never fly again but I forgot I was in Florida now and had to fly back to Texas. Fortunately the flight back to Texas turned out to be non eventful. Nowadays I prefer to drive to Florida or wherever we want to go. I like the feeling of being in control. But in an airplane one has no control. You are at the mercy of the pilot, the engines, technology and the weather. That's too much room for error. Besides when you fly even though it is a convenient way to travel you miss all the sightseeing. And since I love seeing all the sights I think I prefer to drive where I want to go. Of course there could be another occasion when I will have to take flight again. Perhaps I will scarf down a few cocktails at the airport to ease that feeling of being out of control. It's too bad that don't allow smoking on planes anymore. Somehow I think flying and chain smoking would compliment each other very well.

School Days

These next few chapters discuss our school system. I believe that school should be an institution of learning without all the other hoop-la. Our children represent the future and the better educated they are, the better our future. In Texas the homeowners pay school taxes and since I am a homeowner I feel I have the right to voice my opinion. Some may disagree with me, but I don't care because I thinking about the children.

Our Children, Our Future

We dread it, then we look back at those formative years, and we miss it. School provides the basis for our children to develop both intellectually and emotionally as they learn math, reading and social skills. I have so many wonderful memories of my school days, such as art class, all those science experiments I hated doing, embarrassing myself singing in the choir and smoking in the girl's bathroom. But all kidding aside I'm sure if I were to get a second chance I would have been a model student. But we don't get those second chances, do we?

Today is just another hot day in Houston as it is the month of August, and Houston retailers are getting ready to sponsor a "tax free" weekend for shoppers. They started this program many years ago and thus far it has been very successful. The retailers sell certain items such as clothing, school supplies, shoes, eyeglasses and the list goes on, without sales tax. It makes everyone happy. The retailers are happy because they have above average sales, and the buying public is happy as they can save a lot of money on back to school items for their children. Anyways, all the publicity must have inspired me to write about school. The "tax free" weekend was mainly implemented to help low to average income families provide the necessary clothes and school supplies for their children. As I consider this, I have memories of the schools I went to, which were in middle to upper middle class neighborhoods. However, there are many schools in lower class neighborhoods, which do not resemble the schools I went to. These are old, neglected buildings which are outdated and grungy looking. That is the best way I can describe them. Many of them have installed temporary buildings to accommodate their growing classrooms. These old and outdated schools I am referring to are usually located in the poor, crime ridden neighborhoods. Now the children who live in these areas did not ask to be born and raised there, they are victims of their parent's choices or lack of choices. Perhaps their parent's fell into bad times or never had the opportunities the rest of us had. If you go to the more affluent areas of town you will find schools that look more like resort hotels. Wait a minute. What is wrong with this picture? Why should poor children go to their poor schools, while middle class and wealthy children go to their middle class and wealthy schools? Well, I have the solution. The public schools get their funding from the property taxes paid in their districts as I mentioned before. In addition, they get other incentives if the schools rate well on the national test scores for the TAST tests. (I forgot what TAST stands for because it has been so long since I took that stupid test). And it is so dumb. I've heard from my daughter while she was a student teacher that more time is spent in the classroom preparing the children for the "TAST" test, than actually teaching math or spelling. That is because the schools want the children to score well so they receive more funding. This should not be the case. All the property tax money should go into one big pot and be divided equally depending on the enrollment for that particular school. School should be a place to get an education, not a place to socialize by the pool, or to enjoy the indoor botanical gardens while reading in the library. In other words the funding should be divided equally regardless of the district of the school. By doing this each school would have the appropriate funding they need and the children would be the beneficiaries. The TAST test should be abolished so the teachers can start teaching the subjects they're supposed to teach. I don't know if the TAST test is offered in other states but I say the TAST test has failed. It's time to get rid of it once and for all. And if the property taxes were divided equally among all the school districts I'll bet the students at the poor schools would have a better chance to succeed. I say this because those lower class schools would have more money for resources, to hire more staff and offer special programs. Of course it is also up to the parents of the children to do their part. Children need encouragement and involvement from their parents. But once the children arrive at the bus stop it is up to the taxpayers to do their part, and up to the state to give every child an equal chance of success. And we can do this by being fair with the funding so each school get's an equal "slice of the pie" so to speak. So I say let's do away with districting and the TAST test and allocate the property tax earnings based on enrollment, thus giving each child a fair chance. Hey if you don't like my idea there's always private schools available, for those who can afford to send their children to private schools.

Time to Focus on Education

As I mentioned in the previous chapter the money allotted for each school should depend on the enrollment. But I have other suggestions which could change the look and overall function of our public schools. I believe we need to remove all the non-academic programs in the schools. The teachers complain about being underpaid, well, if I had my way, teachers would be some of the highest paid professionals in the nation. And I believe they deserve it, as they are the ones who nurture, inspire and care for our children as we entrust them with our children's care from Pre-K to high school. Teachers set the stage that allows our children to make their dreams and wishes come true. And how much does a dream cost? Remember your favorite teacher? I'm sure almost everyone can remember that one special teacher. So in order to achieve higher salaries for our teachers we should change the focus of our schools. I believe that all extra-curricular activities, including sports, should be removed from the public schools. This includes football, swimming, soccer, hockey, band, cheerleading, well you get the picture. The schools would only teach academic subjects, therefore allowing for a shorter school day. By eliminating sports, band, choir and other elective courses the student would be learning the necessary subjects to prepare them for life in the real world. If the schools were operational for less time they would need less energy and could save money across the board. If needed the schools could offer an additional hour for tutoring or parent teacher conferences. Of course physical education or recess could still be offered to give children a chance to work off some of their energy. So you ask, what about Friday night football? There could still be Friday night football, but it would not be sponsored by the public schools. Rather it would be sponsored by the private sector. The stadiums that are currently owned by the public schools could be sold or leased to private teams formed by the community. Hey, and the money collected from the sale or lease of the stadiums could go back to the schools to provide more computers, books, or whatever they need it for. Education is the foundation of learning that's helps us in the real world, whereas athletics is a pastime. I don't know how sports became such a large part of our education system, but it has now become the spoiled stepchild that has demanded too much time, resources and energy from our schools. The removal of all the extracurricular programs from our public schools could create opportunities for money to be made in the private sector. If there was a demand for privatizing these activities some of you enterprising individuals out there should be thanking me later. I believe our school and government officials should look closely at my idea. They might be amazed at how much money is saved by eliminating the non-academic programs from our schools. The money could then be used towards higher teacher's salaries and as I mentioned before, more money for the classrooms.

I am happy to write that my daughter is now a certified teacher. She has a chance to affect many young lives, and I feel she will do so in a positive way. By removing all the non-academic clutter from the schools such as pep rallies, football and soccer games, swim meets, and so on the children can focus on the true meaning of education, which is the classroom teaching. Our learning institutions can be just that, learning institutions without the all the other hoopla. Sort of like a high tech little red school house where the focus is learning, not playing. It would be a real transition for most, but I believe it would benefit the children. When I think of education I think of math, history, reading and science. Let's face it, being able to run and jump may keep one in shape, but it won't make a child smarter. The objective of education should be learning. Smarter kids equal a better and brighter future for all of us.

Preparatory School

I was thinking about my nephew who will be graduating from high school soon. It seems like yesterday when I went to his first birthday party and he was sitting in his high chair with cake all over his face as he had not yet mastered the spoon. Then I remembered when I graduated from high school many, many years ago. I felt a sense of freedom yet a sense of loneliness and dread at the same time. I imagine I awoke the next morning realizing I was independent now. It was a time of anxiety because I had the whole world at my disposal, but what was I going to do with my life? So I had an idea though which would make the transition a little easier for today's young people. As young people are preparing to graduate, I believe the public school system should offer one year of preparatory school. This program could offer college accredited classes with a combination of teaching life skills and provide career counseling as well. Preparatory school would be part of the public school agenda so there would be no cost or a very minimal cost. The hours would be flexible to accommodate students with working schedules or other responsibilities. Anyone who had graduated from high school would be eligible. I mentioned life skill classes, because let's face it, not every home teaches our children real life skills. What do I mean by life skills? Well, such things as how to balance a check book, how to interview successfully with a company and how to manage a budget. This program could get our young people off to a good start in life. Perhaps there could be classes that teach family planning or how to select a career. This school program could be the missing link between high school and college. There could be a class on how to finance one's college education for those who planned to attend college. And the result would be better informed youth, thus a chance to yield more productive members of our society. I know some of the young people reading this may think it sucks, but it really doesn't. Because those students could still carry on with their life as planned but could elect to attend the preparatory school for a few hours a week. There are many families that can't afford college and as a result their children end up with low paying or mediocre jobs and that trend is passed on to their children, especially with the high cost of college tuition these days. You know I had many dreams when I was in high school, I wanted to be an astronomer, a geologist, a nurse, a French language translator and last but not least, a writer. If you saw that movie "Deep Impact" which was released in 1998, there is a scene where an astronomer was working at an observatory by himself one night. He was eating cold pizza, listening to his favorite music on the loud speakers, and all the while he was looking at pictures of a doomsday asteroid that was sent to him by a boy who was a member of an astronomy club. The boy had discovered the asteroid by accident one night while he was stargazing with his family and friends. Now back to the guy that was working at the observatory. That would be my dream job, working alone in an observatory with the stars above and music filling my head. Well here I am today working for a small company as an office manager. While I love my job it is not my "dream job". If I had gotten a college degree I could have pursued a job that would have been more meaningful and interesting. Now I am too old, I mean too tired to go to college. I make enough money to be comfortable with my life, but I never seem to have the extra money to do the things I really want to do such as travel. Anyways, if I would have had the opportunity of preparatory school who knows, my life could have turned out different? I think whenever our young people graduate from high school they need a sense of direction. The preparatory school could help students find their "niche" in life based on their individual intellect and skills. At the very least our young people could have a choice, whereas now they are simply dropped off after all the graduation festivities, and expected to find their way on that lonely street called "life".

New Year's Eulogy

I am writing this chapter on the eve of a new year. The New Year represents new beginnings and a time to reflect on the year that has just passed. We cannot reclaim the days that have passed, so I think about what I could have done differently. Perhaps this will inspire others to consider their future. First of all I never would have gotten into debt, which thankfully, I have remedied that situation. And I would have gone to college. I married and had children when I was really young, so I could not afford to go to college. But if I had been more determined, I probably could have figured out someway to go. I would have spent more time with my family, because there's no guarantee of tomorrow and I prefer to go through life guiltless whenever I can. I would have prepared more home cooked meals instead of sitting idle at the local fast food drive through restaurant. I would have spent more time talking to my neighbors and less time in front of the television. This would have given me a sense of community as I learned more about my neighbors and their situations. Perhaps I would have visited one of the local churches to check on my relationship with God, just in case he's forgotten that I exist. Now speaking as a woman, I would have kept myself more attractive by dressing better, fixing my hair and wearing make up more often, because first impressions are based on our physical appearance and I'll never know who I could have impressed. I would have allowed more time to start all the projects I wanted to do, instead of waiting for all the tomorrows which came and went without notice, and as a result my projects never got started. I would have visited the graves of my parents more often, because this would have reminded of my love for them, and that life, like all good things, eventually ends. I would have donated my time to help others, even if it seemed inconvenient, because the soul needs nourishment from time to time. I would have walked to the mailbox to retrieve the mail instead of driving to pick up the mail. This way I could have enjoyed the beautiful sky and trees which seem to be more like a painting from the perspective of my indoor window. I would have called my grandchildren more often, just to remind them that I love them and to hear about all their young adventures. But all these things I've mentioned take time and energy, two things they are slowly escaping me as I age. So I will haste to remember all these things before they escape my mind. Because everyday is a new beginning, and I can always do something that will make a difference, regardless of how trivial it seems.

Changing Our Out of Control World

You know we go through life with certain ideals and goals and we get upset when things beyond our control affect us personally. All you have to do is watch the news, crime is getting out of control, illegal drugs are everywhere, and no matter how far away you live from the action, you're simply not safe anymore. My parents never had to install an alarm system in our home, or make sure they locked the car at night, but that innocent age is gone forever. I don't see any light at the end of the tunnel, but perhaps they are some changes we could make that could not only benefit us personally but also change our thought processes. Let's see if change is good, or bad. Well I guess it depends on who you are.

Our Borders and the Swinging Door

Yes I'm on a roll. I live right outside of Houston and the Hispanic population is huge here. I remember back in the 1970's people of Hispanic origin were simply called Mexicans. But now we have to be politically correct and call them Hispanic, whatever. Many of the government officials in Texas cater to the Mexicans because they want the Hispanic vote. As a consequence they are afraid to offend the illegal population because it would not settle well the legal Hispanic voters. Of course out of all the Mexican population I imagine only half of them are here legally and thus able to vote.

We are being bombarded by illegal Mexicans as they are starting to invade every aspect of our lives. I remember many years ago when you saw people walking down the street it meant they were poor or homeless. Now there are herds of Mexicans wondering our streets usually on foot or riding bicycles. They do this because they cannot obtain a drivers license. I have even seen them coming from the woods, which leads me to believe they sleep in the woods! These are not people, they are animals. Now I'm not referring to the sophisticated, educated legal Mexicans who are productive members of our society. I am referring to the dusty, unshaven men I see coming from the woods. I've seen trucks stopping on the side of the road to pick these men up to offer jobs for low pay. Now if I can spot them why can't the officials spot them? Look I understand these illegal Mexicans want to make their life better, but they're doing it at the expense of taxpayers like you and me. Who do you think pays for their medical care? We do. Who do you think pays for their ride back to Mexico when they are apprehended by the police or immigration bureau? We do. Who do you think pays for their children's schooling? We do. Who do you think pays for their time in jail or prison when they commit crimes? We do. They compromise our safety as many of them resort to crime when they are not able to find work and we are the victims. Well I would like to be in charge of this problem for one week. First of all I would encourage the government to publicize a toll free phone number that the public could call to report illegal immigrants especially those who are in the work force illegally. Once they called they would be issued a case number if the information was worthy of investigating. If the illegal immigrant was picked up and processed the person who called in would receive a monetary reward. I guarantee the phones would be ringing off the wall. Of course the caller would remain anonymous so there would not be any consequence for the caller. Once the illegal's immigrants were brought in they would be turned over to the immigration office. At the immigration office they would be photographed, finger printed and samples of their DNA would be taken. I mentioned the DNA sampling because who knows what crimes or devious deeds they may have done? Some people would feel that this practice of getting their DNA would be inhumane. But if they are not here legally, they don't have any rights to speak of. Now if the offenders were caught a second time there would be a record of their prior occupation and they could be dealt with as a repeat offender. The fact that these illegal immigrants take advantage of what our society has to offer really disturbs me. They overpopulate our cities and take jobs away from our citizens. In addition to all this if an illegal immigrant gives birth to their child in the U.S. that child is considered a legal citizen. The illegal immigrants know about this law and I feel that take advantage of it. The law should be amended in a way that if a child is born of illegal immigrants the hospital paperwork would show "non-citizen". But in all fairness if one parent is a legal citizen then the child should have the same rights. This act alone could save our government millions of dollars which currently goes to raising these children. That is why I like my idea of getting the public involved and believe me they would do it for the small reward I mentioned. Our government needs to take action, or if they will not take action just remove all the border patrols and put up big signs saying "Welcome to America". Supposedly Texas won its independence from Mexico back in 1836. Or did we? Ironically the final battle happened at a place call "San Jacinto", which is located right outside of Houston. If you were to go to that place right now you would probably find illegal Mexicans somewhere in the vicinity, perhaps enjoying a picnic on the fields of that famous place where our ancestors fought. So maybe we won the battle, but not the war.

The Un-united States of America

For God sakes, let's have a national driver's license! We live in a transit society, not like the old days where you were born, raised and died in the same community. People are changing jobs all the time, seeking new places to live, and our government makes it a challenge to move from one state to another because you must get a drivers license for each state you choose to live in. So I suggest we have a national driver's license. If there's going to be a so called "national" driver's license, there would need to be a national database to store all the information. Right now each state has to share information as the databases are set up state to state. But imagine if there was only one database, the records would be readily available for law enforcement. A bar code on the license could be scanned to reveal that's person's driving record, and perhaps we could go a step further and have other information listed such as blood type or medical information, and criminal records. Now the law enforcer would have a record of that person's history in one swipe of the bar code. I know some people out there believe this would be an invasion of their civil rights, but if they are not criminals why should they care? The bar code would be discreet and if you're in an accident it would be great if a paramedic could know that you're diabetic or have some illness where you might need to be treated differently. Maybe the medical information could be provided on a voluntary basis in case certain individuals didn't want to share their medical history.

Now I don't think violent criminals who have served time or been on probation should have the right to drive. What I mean is if a convicted felon is released from prison then he or she should not be able to get a drivers license ever! Let's face it, many criminals cannot get jobs because they have a criminal record, therefore they become repeat offenders. By letting criminals drive just gives them access to do more crimes, like drive to a bank to rob it, or drive around to sell drugs. Do you think they should have that right? To better explain let's say a felon who has served their sentence is released from prison. If that felon committed a violent crime, meaning they used physical force or weapons, they would not be eligible to receive or renew their driver's license. I'm pretty sure a felon can't buy a gun, so why should they be able to get a drivers license? I believe the practice of having court approval to reinstate one's driver's license should go into effect for all criminals once they are released from prison or have served probation. Because I believe if you are convicted of any crime, you should immediately be stripped of all your rights, until your sentence is completed. Let's make it hard on criminals so they have to become accountable for their actions. With the national driver's license, your records go with you whoever, or wherever you are in this great country. And with the national database to support the national driver's license I believe America will finally be united, at least when it comes to driving across the state line. The national driver's license would basically look the same as the current driver's license and the bar code could yield criminal backgrounds, driving records and perhaps medical information. I think it would also be a good idea to list an emergency contact person in case of an accident so someone could be notified immediately. Of course the emergency contact information could also be optional. We live in the super computer age and I think our nation could easily make this transition even if it is only one state at a time. I say let them start with Texas. It's about time we start making positive changes and simplifying the way we do things in this great country. And I'm not just referring to the idea of a national driver's license. There are many changes that could be made nationwide as opposed to statewide. It's about time we all got on the same page.

The World is Our Prison

You know, war sucks. But it is one of those consequences of human nature. It is in our blood, literally, as our ancestors have indulged in the practice of war over and over. And I guess we will never learn how to live peacefully on this beautiful planet as long as there is something to fight about. So we depend on our military might to protect us. Many civilians who sign up to join the military do so for the benefits and the training. It is a good way to learn a career if you are disciplined enough to be a soldier. My oldest son is a Sergeant in the U.S. Army. I am very proud of his service, which includes one year in Iraq. Thankfully he returned home without incident, but there were some close calls. Needless to say I was a nervous wreck the whole time he was over there. His wife and my daughter in law, managed to take care of their three children during his absence, and I don't know how she did it. She is a real trooper. But there are many unfortunate souls in the prime of their lives who do not return home to their families. God Bless them all and I hope their families know they died honorably. Now on the other end of humanity, we have a dark side, which is our criminal population. One night my husband and I were watching a documentary about prisons, and the light came on. The show was talking about overcrowded prisons and portrayed most of the inmates as being violent and rebellious. After the show was over my husband and I discussed the idea about criminals being enlisted in the military. If they want to fight, let's give them a time and a place to do so. Let's send them to the front lines of war, I mean let's give them an ultimatum which could include military service as opposed to serving jail time for their crimes. These are young, fit and mostly intelligent individuals who have made mistakes in their lives for whatever reason. But they could also be a valuable resource by serving in the military and by doing so the taxpayers would be getting something back for their hard earned money. My idea is a program that would allow convicted criminals to serve in the military in replacement of their sentence. I feel there are certain criminals who would not be eligible for such a program such as convicted murderers, child molesters or rapists. But for someone who is serving time for less intimidating crimes, they could be given an option to serve military time. If these criminals were given a choice and they accepted the military sentence, they would have to pass a physical, then off to boot camp. Here is how it would work, the convicted criminal would stand in front of the judge and receive their sentence of prison time, or as an alternative, the judge could offer them a military sentence, if certain qualifications were met. It would all depend on the type of crime committed, the prisoner's age and their physical and mental health. If the convicted offender selected the military sentence they would have to serve the sentence flawlessly and upon receiving their honorable discharge from the military, their criminal case would be dismissed. I think a fair military sentence would be to serve two to five years depending on the offense they committed. Once they completed their military sentence the offender would simply present their honorable discharge to the presiding court, and they would be free to go. This would not only lower the prison population but it might, just might rehabilitate the criminals and make them worthy of rejoining our society. If however a criminal who had elected to take the military sentence failed to commit to their duty and became a problem, they would go right back to the courts. These less hardened criminals would receive pay but their pay would be less than those in the regular service and the benefits would also be reduced. In addition there would be a badge or some identification showing they are part of the prison military branch. This would be for the safety of their military comrades serving alongside them. But if the offender had served a military sentence and received an honorable discharge, they could opt to rejoin the military as a civilian, and their record of service could be transferred so they become eligible for full pay and benefits. This concept reminds me of a movie called "The Dirty Dozen", but on a much larger scale. (The "Dirty Dozen" was based loosely on the same concept, of prisoners being able to serve in battle. It made a big hit when released back in 1967). You know we all make mistakes in our lives, some of us just make bigger mistakes, or should I say, some just get caught. I believe this program could help reform some of those that made mistakes in their lives. In addition it could also increase our military power without the hefty price tag of trying to enlist more civilians. And I would rather see my tax dollars going to a productive cause, such as protecting my country, as opposed to paying for inmates to have cable TV in their cell. And in this day and time, with all the threats to our peaceful existence in this uncertain world we live in, I might just sleep a little better at night knowing that our military could be more powerful than ever. I think this idea is a win, win situation for all concerned, except for our enemies of course.

Cat Schmidt

Smoking Section

By now I'm sure you have probably figured out that I am a smoker. While I'm not proud of the fact, it is something I must deal with. Thankfully I am not one of those "three pack a day" smokers, or chain smokers. Rather I am a structured smoker. I have set aside certain times of the day for my nicotine addiction such as I generally smoke with my first cup of coffee, second cup of coffee, after lunch, before dinner, after dinner and before bedtime. Of course I cannot smoke at my office where I work, but I do remember the good old days when I used to smoke at the office. I would have the phone in one hand as I discussed business with an unsuspecting customer and my cigarette in the other hand. It almost seems like an illusion now. I also used to smoke in my vehicle, but that changed when my husband and I bought a new truck many years ago. I agreed not to smoke in the truck and never have to this day. I remember when I used to own a car which had a five speed transmission, you know the kind you have to manually shift, and I used to smoke in that vehicle. Somehow I could juggle my cigarette, drink and shift gears all at the same time. Now I drive the truck I mentioned earlier and it is has an automatic transmission. It would make it much easier to juggle my cigarette and drink while I'm driving but remember I made the vow not to smoke in that vehicle. Ironic isn't it? Now my husband is not a smoker so I try not to expose him to second hand smoke. At home I smoke outside. However there is the occasional trip to our local restaurant, and thankfully my husband doesn't mind if we sit in the smoking section. I guess this is my reward for not smoking in the house or the vehicle. It never fails that shortly after we are seated at the restaurant, here comes a family with their children. I know it's probably second nature for that family to bring their young children into the smoking section, but somehow I don't feel it is right. I mean you see the family sit down with the small child or infant, and then light up. What is wrong with that picture? Well, first of all there should be a law that prohibits young children from being seated in the smoking section of any restaurant or establishment that has a smoking section. I can hear all the cheering as you read that last statement. Back to my point, since the parents or family of that child do not have the consideration not to smoke around them, I believe the lawmakers should intercede. It is a known fact that second hand smoke can affect one's health. And children have smaller lungs than adults, which could make them even more susceptible to the smoke. Let's face it, with children it may be difficult to tell how old they are. And since children generally do not carry identification, how one would know how old they are? I would venture to say that any child who is under the age of eighteen should not be allowed into a smoking section. Now there are some fourteen years old that look like they're eighteen the way they dress and the way the girls wear make up. I guess if the parents want to be devious about their children's age there is nothing one could do. I imagine one day there will not be a smoking section, and probably sooner than later, but until that day let's protect the innocents from being subjected to cigarette smoke. You see, I can be rational if I want to be. Now get the fuck out of my face, I will quit when I am ready.

Remote Control World

It wasn't easy to think of a title for this chapter. I was going to call it "Mr. Remote Control", but changed my mind at the last minute, just as my husband changes the TV channels. You find them in every home, rich or poor; it doesn't matter, if you own a television or any other electronics chances are you own a remote control device. I think it was a good invention. I remember when I was younger; whenever my Dad wanted to change the channel on our retro television set he reluctantly got off the couch, walked slowly to the TV, and turned the knob to the channel he wanted. Back in those days everyone watched the commercials, because you wouldn't want to keep getting up and down to change the channel every time a commercial came on. Beside there were only a few channels to select from back in those days. But that was then, this is now. Today we live in a society of convenience, pushing a button can make our life easier, thus the remote control. However, there are those who abuse this privilege to some degree, such as my husband. As soon as we get home from work or wherever, he sits in his comfy chair and grabs for the remote. This way he is assured to be in control of the TV, and I am at the wrath of his channel surfing. My husband never accesses the TV guide station, which could help him to select which program he would like to watch. He prefers to flip through all the stations, back and forth, over and over, until it reaches a point that I am starring at the walls and ceilings. I'll be watching a glimpse of the many programs that appear, and say "oh, that's a good show", and before I know it, it's gone. He resumes his passion of flipping again, I see another good program, "oh, can we watch that?" I say, and before I can finish my sentence, it's gone. What's really frustrating is when we both find a program we want to watch, and begin watching it, then the commercials come on, and you guessed it, my husband begins his channel flipping. A few moments later I ask, "Where is the program we were watching?" and my husband replies, "I'm trying to find it." This means he didn't notice which channel the program was on, and by the time he finds it we've missed a good portion of the show. There have been times when my husband flipped through so many channels that I started to get nauseated. I don't think the human brain is conditioned for this type of torture. By the time you get your eyes and ears focused on the screen, the image is gone and in a millisecond it is replaced with another image. There have also been times when my husband was not around and I decided to watch TV, but guess what, I couldn't find the damned remote. Now I'm not going to walk up to the TV, and turn it on manually, instead I start searching for my husband. I might have to walk outside, down the street, or to the backyard, but I will eventually find my husband. Once I do find him, he looks at me as if I've been stalking him. As I approach him with my look of frustration he looks down on me with a hint of guilt, and says "What?" I reply, "Where is the damned remote?" Then he grabs the remote from his pocket, acting like he didn't know how it got there, and hands it to me. The remote is like an extension of his body which he covets and keeps securely attached to his being. Scientist should figure out a way to implant remotes so people could just blink, or move a finger to change the channels. Hum, that reminds me of a TV program I used to like called "Bewitched". Anyways, you haven't seen anything till you see my husband perform with multiple remote controls. Imagine it is our weekly party night and we begin to listen to music, which my husband controls with the remote control to the CD player. But there is another remote control for the other CD player that is connected to the surround sound, thus two remote controls. Later my husband may decide to play a music DVD, and has to use a third remote control for the DVD player. Last but not least there is a remote for the turntable. So here sits my husband, after a few drinks, trying to maneuver with three or four remote controls, and keep the music and TV going all at the same time. I sit back and watch the show in amazement. I don't know how he manages the juggling act. But all good things have to come to an end, and when it's all over, the remote controls are returned to their resting place, and the house is eerily quite, which in a way is kind of nice.

Know Thy Neighbor

You know I watch so much news related to terrorists and their resolve to kill innocent people that it makes me sick. Sometimes the news anchor talks about the possibility of terrorists living in the United States. This reminds me of a movie called "Alien" from 1979. I enjoy watching sci-fi thrillers and this movie is a classic in that category. The movie takes place in outer space as a small crew is on a mining exploration to mine other planets. There is a scene where the space explorers set their spacecraft down on an unfamiliar planet because they are receiving some kind of beacon from their communications. The crew discovers an alien spacecraft that had crashed on the planet sometime ago and they set out to explore the craft. One of the crew members discovers some eggs on the alien craft that are alive and as a result an alien parasite attaches to his face. The crew heads back to their ship and Sigourney Weaver who plays a character named Ripley, will not allow the crew back on the ship for fear of being contaminated by the alien parasite. There is a science officer who is on board the ship who overrides Ripley's decision and lets the crew aboard. Now the parasite is still attached to the crew member's face but eventually removes itself and is killed. But the crew finds out later that the alien had implanted another creature inside the crew member which eventually becomes a full grown alien monster. There is one point in the movie where Ripley questions the science officer about breaking the rules and letting the contaminated space explorer back on the ship. The science officer is examining the parasite specimen which they killed earlier as he comments to Ripley about his scientific findings about the creature. Ripley replies to the science officer, as she sarcastically rebuttals him saying, *"And you let it in"*, referring to the alien creature. I love that famous line because Sigourney Weaver says it so perfectly. And what is my point you may ask? Well, we could be saying that same line to our government, except we would have to say, *"And you let them in"*, referring to the terrorists. I would refer to the terrorists as the "parasite" and they could be planning to implant a weapon of mass destruction while we are going about our daily routines. I know our government is taking steps to secure our borders, but I believe they need to do more. First of all certain countries such as Iran, Pakistan, North Korea and Syria should be on a list of hostile countries and people from those countries should not be allowed to visit or obtain visa's to stay in our country. I believe we should not "let them in". The list of so called "hostile countries" should be updated on a regular basis by our government. Secondly anyone from one of those countries who is visiting or already living here should be deported. I know that is extreme but those who are deported can blame their country for their indisposition, and not the United States. This would also send a message to those hostile countries that we, the United States, or getting very strict about our security. We must also secure our borders with some sort of barrier. I know this would be a major and costly endeavor, but we must do it. Why don't we use the prison population as a labor force? We could even pay them a salary which could be deposited in their prison bank account to go into an education fund. We must also keep tabs on any visitors that are already here. When a foreigner visits they should be required to go through the homeland security office which could have substations set up at all airports and shipping docks. The visitors could be required to report the length of their stay, where they will be visiting and the name and address of anyone they are visiting. If their visit is longer than two weeks they should report to a local government office every thirty days for the duration of their stay. Failure to do this would result in a warrant for their arrest and eventual deportation. Right now there are millions of illegal immigrants living here from Mexico. The terrorists probably observe how relaxed our security is and laugh at our system. If our government cannot control the onslaught of illegal immigrants from Mexico, then what can the government control? The government must get serious and start acting instead of spending time discussing the situation. I feel that time is not on our side. It has been too many years since that terrible attack on 9-11-2001 and it is just a matter of time before America is assaulted again. I also believe we are sending too many troops to foreign countries when we need them here to protect our own country. I understand the war in Afghanistan is ongoing, and the middle east is very volatile and always will be, but our military has done its job overseas. If the United States needs a presence in those countries we could keep a couple of active military basis open for good gesture, but that would be the extent of our involvement. If the people of Iraq and Afghanistan want to self destruct, so be it. And as for Afghanistan, how can our soldiers fight a war when they can't even recognize the enemy? I believe the war in Afghanistan should be fought by intelligence and not on the ground. Of course I realize that Iraq provides us oil, one of those spoils of war, so we could maintain a military base next to the precious oil if needed. These dumb ass terrorists spend all their time and energy thinking of ways to infiltrate our country and do damage. They are living in a religious and fanatical pipe dream which has become more like a nightmare to the rest of the world. I don't understand why we can't just get along, but I guess we are passed that point. But there is one thing we can do. First of all, get rid of the Department of Immigration". Let the "Department of Homeland Security" be in charge of anyone who is trying to come to the US. Anyone who is a foreigner would be scrutinized by the "Department of Homeland Security". No more playing footsies with the "Department of Immigration". I also believe the airlines must do their part. There should be a federal law for all incoming flights that passengers can only have one carry on bag and it must be a clear plastic bag. This way the contents would be visible for airport security and make their job easier. The clear bags could be purchased at the airports if needed. Furthermore the airlines would not allow other baggage to be carried on the same flight as the passengers. The baggage would be carried on a separate flight for baggage only. It may cause a little inconvenience but most of the time the baggage would arrive around the same time as the passengers. Lastly I believe Americans can do their part by keeping a watchful eye on their neighbors and other people in their communities. I believe there should be a national toll free phone number anyone could call to report a suspicious person or incident to. This toll free number could be publicized to the masses over and over. If certain ethnic groups don't like it, that's too fucking bad. After all, we didn't start this religious war, they did. I know America is known as the "melting pot" for all nationalities but the innocence of that glorious past age is gone. America must get tough with their policy and keep a watchful eye on whoever enters our country. Right now the United States imposes trade embargos as tactics to scare other nations. But embargos don't work, as other countries do not have the same intentions and trade continues with those countries. A good example is Cuba. They trade freely with Europe, Canada and other countries. Personally I think we should be friendly with Cuba. Whatever they did back in the 1960's should be forgiven by now, that was another age and the so called radical leader of that time is now an old man, namely Castro. In this day and time we need more friends than enemies, so I think we should lift the embargo on Cuba. Just a thought, besides it would be a nice place to vacation. And how long does the United States have to hold a grudge? I believe it all goes back to bureaucracy which we have too much of. I think it's time to stop talking and start acting, before it's too late for us all.

Taxes and Health Insurance Reform

The dreaded tax season is upon us as I am writing these chapters in the month of February. It is cold, windy and gloomy outside. I haven't worn my sunglasses in a least of couple of weeks now. I know people in general don't like to discuss taxes or insurance. It is sort of a forbidden subject yet we all have to do the inevitable which is to file our tax return, or do we? The next chapters will discuss that prospect along with some alternatives to help people become medically insured.

Death by Taxation

Well, the New Year has arrived, and everyone knows that the dreadful tax season looms in the future. It is that grueling formality that Americans face every year, sort of like your annual dental check up. But despite the dread of it, it is our duty to pay taxes. So the W-2's start arriving in the mail or at the workplace, then the government income tax forms invade the local post offices by the truckloads. It is really sickening. No let me rephrase that, it is really dumb! Everyone in America is going to have to pay taxes if they didn't contribute enough through their incomes and the rest of us will receive some sort of refund if we overpaid. It is an endless see-saw ride and we're all on it together. Well, I think there is a remedy. It is ... are you ready? The flat tax, or consumer tax, as proposed by politicians before.

Look, we have to pay taxes. That is what keeps our country running. But what about all the people who don't pay taxes or pay very little taxes, such as the illegal aliens, the people who find loopholes or those who are simply dishonest? Well, it's just not fair. My solution will make it easy for the government to collect taxes, and the best part is one will not have to worry about the so called "easy form", or is it the "E-Z" form, that is not so easy to fill out. That form along with all the other confusing forms, would be history. You would not be penalized if you are married and have to pay more taxes. This tax would be an equal tax regardless of status, age or income. Now there is one thing that really bugs me, we pay income tax, social security tax, Medicare tax, sales tax and if you drink alcohol or smoke, you pay additional taxes when you buy liquor or cigarettes. Plus there's the tax on gasoline, which no one can avoid if you want to drive. And if you are a homeowner, there may be property tax, plus school and MUD taxes. My proposal with the flat tax, would streamline most of these tax entities, and would simplify the whole process of paying taxes. The date of April 15th would no longer be associated with the mad rush to the post office to mail in your IRS payment, but rather April 15th would be just another spring day. So here we go, the good news is that when you receive your hard earned paycheck, there would be no tax deducted, which means you get to keep all of your money. However there is a flipside. Whenever you purchase something, rather it be a package of gum or a new car, you are going to pay the "flat tax" which contributes money to the government for all the various taxes. Without the flat tax a pack of gum might cost around $1.00 plus sales tax. Locally I would pay about a $1.07 for the pack of gum including sales tax. With the flat tax added that same pack of gum could cost significantly more, maybe as much as $1.20 including the flat tax and sales tax. Not so bad you may say, but apply that same tax to a new car purchase, or maybe a new washing machine and the price tag will go up astronomically. But remember, you get to keep your whole paycheck to start off with. Most Americans are not wealthy, we're just trying to pay our bills and maybe enjoy a few small luxuries. If you spend less money, you would pay less tax. Those who are wealthy, who spend more, would pay more tax. And that's just the way it is, like it or not. The beauty of this plan is that each individual could decide what is affordable, and maybe save up a little extra before they buy that new boat, because they would have to consider how much the boat would cost with the new flat tax. In other words, we the people would be in control of our tax spending, not the government. Remember I had referred to the illegal aliens who obviously don't pay taxes? Their employers know their situation and pay the workers cash and of course their wages are never reported to the government. Well with the flat tax they would pay taxes too, rather they like it or not. Basically if you buy something, you are contributing to the national tax effort. The government could figure out how to divvy up all the tax money and I think they're pretty good at that. Of course there are some things that should never be taxable such as food, prescription drugs, medical care, baby diapers, insurance, retirement investing, let me repeat, retirement investing. I also believe that resale items should not be taxed. These are items such as clothes purchased in resale shops, items purchased in pawn shops, used cars, boats and motorcycles, used furniture and so on. Well you get the idea. Tax was paid on these items when they were purchased new so why should we have to pay tax on those items a second time? It seems as though the government is double dipping. Now back to the flat tax, imagine no more tax forms, no more deadlines, no more trying to figure out how to get a bigger tax refund, or to scramble for more tax deductions. The government wouldn't be laughing at your tax return because you missed a deduction you never knew about. Now if you own property you would still receive a tax bill for property taxes because that would be considered an individual tax. Now I've saved the best for last. Just imagine how much paper could be recycled if we got rid of all those income tax forms. Isn't it glorious? We could have one hell of a bonfire. No, I'm just kidding. I believe that paper should be recycled. You see, I believe that life is too complicated. The flat tax would simplify how we pay taxes. There would be an added benefit to employers as well, as they would not need to figure out how much tax to deduct from your paycheck. Now companies and corporations may still have to file tax forms and figure out deductions but the rest of us could enjoy the benefits of a flat tax. Just imagine, on April 14th, everyone can sleep peacefully instead of staying up all night trying to finagle numbers around on those damned tax forms. But don't write your congress representative yet, because it won't do any good. I suggest the next time you file your tax return you get a marker and write with big letters, "I want the flat tax"! Maybe if enough people do this, the IRS will get the picture.

Dying to Get Medical Insurance?

I remember when I was growing up with my brothers and sisters there were plenty of times when we went to the doctor or emergency room. When I was about six years old my father, mother and younger brother were involved in an auto accident which severely injured both my parents. Thankfully they both made a full recovery but if that same accident had occurred in today's world, the costs for their recovery would have been monumental. Back then my father had medical insurance through his job, and it was sufficient enough to pay for all our medical needs, and it didn't cost that much. Nowadays there are thousands of people without medical insurance coverage, due to the fact that medical insurance is too expensive, or maybe our money just doesn't go as far. I think it is both of these reasons. So what does one do? Well, I don't really have a good answer, but one thing I do know is that medical insurance companies pay millions of dollars for fraudulent claims every year and we pay the price. I've seen those nightly news shows on TV where people submit claims for medical care they never received, or doctor's falsified patient records so they could get payment from Medicaid, Medicare or individual health care polices. First of all these individuals need to be prosecuted big time. I'm talking the Enron scale of punishment. But that's just part of the problem. The medical clinics and hospitals are also guilty. I believe they rake up the charges by doing unnecessary tests and procedures, and then overcharge for their services. Let's face it everyone wants a piece of the pie. I understand that hospitals and doctors want to make money, and they should be profitable, but not at the expense of people having to go through life without medical insurance. So how do we fix the problem?

First of all I believe that all companies who offer medical insurance should have to inform potential new hires at the time they are offered a job, of their insurance benefits. By doing that the potential new hire can decide if the medical insurance benefits would meet their needs and if not they could look elsewhere for employment. When someone is employed they should have a choice of the type of medical coverage offered by the company. For instance if a young, healthy employee doesn't feel they would need medical care too often they could opt for a medical plan that only covers emergency care or hospitalization. An older employee would probably want full coverage. I believe there should be different medical plans made available depending on the needs of the individual. This could be an incentive that companies could offer their employees. Now if you work for a small company, you're just SOL, because you're going to pay out of your ass for insurance benefits, or they may not offer insurance benefits at all. This leads me to my next suggestion. The insurance companies have to pay the claims, and are very stringent about their spending. So why don't they open medical clinics? That way that could hire the medical staff and all the money would go right into their pockets. The patients, who are already paying premiums to that insurance company, could receive care at a reduced cost. I'm not going to name names, but say for instance you are insured by ABC medical insurance. ABC would open clinics in the major cities, and if you should need medical care, you could go to the clinic down the street and pay their prices, or you could drive a little further and go to the ABC clinic and pay a reduced price because you are already an insured member. I think this would work for routine medical care and non emergencies. It would also eliminate fraudulent practices, because the care is being provided directly from the insurance company and their clinics. But what if the company you work for doesn't offer ABC medical insurance? Well, you could apply for insurance directly at the ABC clinic, where you would pay a monthly premium. You would be issued a private sector insurance card, and could receive medical care at a reduced rate when needed. Sort of like an insurance credit card. Another thought is medical insurance companies could offer hospitalization coverage only, and one would pay a lower cost for the premium. This way you may have to pay out of pocket for a doctor's visit but in the event you are hospitalized, you are covered. You know it just takes a little imagination and planning, and I don't know what the big deal is. I don't foresee any big changes in the future, but employers could look at different ways to offer medical insurance as I discussed before. One thing that really pisses me off is that temporary and part time employees are usually not offered medical insurance benefits. I believe the lawmakers need to change this. These contract workers deserve benefits too! Somehow these companies fell through the benefit's loophole because they do not hire full time employees. Why I ask? Another problem is that most companies have a ninety day waiting period before new hires are eligible for benefits. There should be no waiting period. Here's the way it should go, one applies for a job with a new company. That company would be required by law to provide a written outline of any insurance benefits they offer. They would not have to reveal the name of the provider, but simply what percentage of insurance they offer to the employee, such as 60/40, which translates to the company paying 60% of the benefits, while the employee pays 40%. This information would be made available to any applicant so they could decide if they want to work for this company, or seek work somewhere else. Also, I vote that the ninety day waiting period be abolished. What if one gets really sick during that ninety day period? Let's face it, the medical insurance crisis will not be resolved overnight, but the government and private industries need to do something quick. Oh and one more thing. The high cost of prescription drugs is a sick person's worst nightmare. The pharmaceutical companies are raking it in, and laughing all the way to the bank while someone's dear grandmother can't afford their prescription drugs. First of all the government needs to regulate the price of prescription drugs and all those lobbyists for the drug companies need to be kicked out of Washington. Secondly there should be prescription drug insurance policies for people who require the drugs for long term illnesses such as diabetes, cancer, heart disease and so on. These patients would pay a small premium to get their drugs at a very, reduced cost. You know other countries offer free medical care for their citizens so I don't understand why health care has turned into such a crisis situation right in our own backyard. I believe it is due to greed, a lack of leadership and downright neglect of our government officials. Well someone needs to fix it, and fix it soon. I personally believe that socialized medicine is the answer, but it probably won't happen in my lifetime or as long as the lobbyists that represent the healthcare industry and pharmaceutical companies are paying the lawmakers under the table. Last but not least I believe the government should raise the income standards for Medicaid. This would allow more children to be covered. And the so called illegal immigrants who do not report their wages should not be eligible for Medicaid or any other government based programs. Because if we give the illegal immigrants medical coverage that would be the same as socialized medicine. If the illegal immigrants can qualify, then everyone should qualify. So we must draw the line somewhere. The real sickness is that our government officials are simply not focused on the issues regarding health reform and you and I are going to pay the price.

Out of Control

There are some things in life we have no control over, such as the weather. Then there are things that we would like to change in our society, but there is too much bureaucracy for one person to make a change. However, when it comes to things like conserving energy, recycling and preparing for the storms of life so to speak, one person can make a difference. I believe we just need to be more focused on what is going on around us.

The Weather Channel

I just remembered one of my obsessions, the "Weather Channel". Let's face it we all have our little obsessions or the things in life that make us happy in a strange but fascinating way. One of my obsessions is the weather channel. It all started when I was very young, my father used to go outside at the approach of a storm, and stand on the porch to watch the storm materialize. Being a young girl, I would follow my father outside to observe with him. He would stand there in wonder until the approaching storm was close by. Then he would usher me into the house. He taught me many weather related things such as to how to watch the barometer, and how to recognize a really bad storm. My father became child like as he heard the distant thunder and it was just a matter of time before he would go outside to gauge the storms intensity. That was many years ago when I enjoyed watching the weather with my father, now my husband follows me as I am the one that goes outside and observes the approaching storm. Sometimes I run back into the house, yelling, I have to get the camera, when I see weather that is worthy of my amateur photography. My husband replies, "Oh God, there she goes". Nowadays with the Weather Channel I can monitor the weather all across the country, and watch how the weather affects everyone. One day my husband left the house to run an errand or two, as I was tuned into the Weather Channel station. He came home a couple of hours later and I was still watching the Weather Channel. He remarked "How can anyone watch the weather channel for two hours?" So I had to plead guilty. But weather is so, well, unpredictable. I think that is what makes it so fascinating. Maybe because my life is so predictable, it is nice to relate to something that is not predictable. And besides, someone has to be up to speed with all the weather changes we are going through due to global warming. Even my husband is involved in my following of the global warming trend. If you don't believe we are experiencing global warming, you are very naive. In Houston, Texas it seems that the winter season is getting shorter and shorter. The months of January and February feel more like springtime. I'll be sitting outside on the patio listening to the birds singing, wearing a short sleeve shirt with the sun warming my shoulder then all of a sudden I remember it's the month of January. I don't know how global warming will affect us, but I know it will in some way. All the cheap talk in Washington will not be able to save us, as I am afraid we have acted too late to stop global warming. And besides, if global warming was caused by industrialization and fossil fuel emissions, how is the whole world going to fix the problem? Simply stated they are not. Perhaps nature will resolve the problem, as it has done in the past. All I can say I hope we didn't mess things up too bad for our grandchildren and great grandchildren. And I guess global warming is just another good excuse for me to enjoy watching the Weather Channel. I just wish my father was here to enjoy it with me.

It is Hot or Is It Just Me?

If you haven't had a chance to watch Al Gore's movie documentary titled "An Inconvenient Truth", you should. Rather you are on the global warming band wagon or not, it is worth watching. According to Mr. Gore the world is really warming up on a scale that isn't healthy for the planet or its inhabitants, which includes us humans. Now parts of the presentation may be a little boring as Mr. Gore uses a lot of charts and graphs to get his point across, sort of like my high school science teacher, but overall the documentary is well presented. Mr. Gore makes some powerful points in the documentary, such as Greenland is basically starting to melt, parts of the Artic and Antarctic are dropping into the sea, and there's much more. But you know everything in the documentary is based on science and facts. The movie definitely had an impact on me as it was like watching science fiction but global warming is really happening, so I guess one could call it science non-fiction. According to Mr. Gore we don't have much time to address this problem of global warming. In fact it's probably already too late to reverse the effects of greenhouse gases. Wherever you live in this world, unless you've been living in a cave, chances are you have noticed some subtle or not so subtle climate changes in your locality. For instance in December 2006, it was warm in Houston, Texas. By January some of the plant species were actually sprouting buds. It was like spring time in January. Then there were the April snowstorms of 2007 up north that took everyone by surprise, and we had a second bout of winter. Except it wasn't wintertime, in fact it was in the middle of April. I had to get my jacket out of retirement and wear it as the northern winds came back with a vengeance. But you see, everything is out of whack with the weather. I don't know if one can attribute 100 per cent to global warming, or if we're just going through other climate changes, perhaps it could be a little bit of both scenarios. Another fact that was discussed in the documentary was the population of the world. There are too many people on the planet, and we are using up all the resources. With modern industry we are also polluting the atmosphere, thus global warming. The government doesn't want to fix the problem, because they are part of the problem. By the time the government gets off its big fat ass and does something, it will be too late. In a sense we are all guilty. We buy the cars that use the fossil fuels and the car manufacturers keep on making them, so it's a vicious cycle. The auto makers could make an engine that doesn't need fossil fuels to make it run, but they're all in bed with the oil companies, so they don't want too. Oh sure they act like they want to do something about the problem, but it's all a hype. So you may ask at this point, what can I do to help the problem? Well, first of all think about how you drive. If everyone could plan their driving so they would drive less, that would help a little. For instance, stop at the bank or the grocery store on your way home from work. And if you live in a neighborhood that has stores nearby, try walking for a change. You don't have to drive everywhere. Or ride a bicycle to the neighborhood mailboxes to check your mail. Another big problem is commercialism. It seems like every square inch is being used for new construction. You're probably familiar with those strip shopping centers that consists of four or five different retailers, well they're all over the place and they keep building more. If I drive a few miles down the road, I see vacant buildings with signs that say "available for lease", but if I drive a little further there is new construction for the same type of retail stores. I don't' get it. Why would a retailer want to build a new building when they could occupy a building that's already built? I think the government should put a big tax on new construction for retailers so they will be forced to think about occupying existing buildings. And why for God's sake do they have to cut down all the trees when they build new construction? Why can't they build around the trees? The trees provide a natural barrier against wind, and also provide a home for wildlife. Plus trees are nice to look at. But I've noticed whenever they do new construction, they cut down all the big, beautiful trees, and after the construction is done, they plant new young trees. It doesn't make any sense. People, we are going to pay the price for all this convenience, and for not paying attention to our government's 'Do nothing' attitude. So, if you get a chance watch the documentary, you may or may not be inspired, but chances are it will affect you in some way. Just remember the next time you wear your shorts outside and it is wintertime, you were warned. Or when the sea level rises and your home that was ten miles from the beach is now considered to be beach front property, remember you were warned. Or when you are old, and you can't go outside because the temperature is 120 degrees, remember you were warned. Now I have one more idea that might help the planet. Since we have to keep using conventional fuel for our automobiles, why doesn't someone invent a filter that goes inside the exhaust pipe? The filter would convert the exhaust vapors into liquid form so the exhaust particles would not go into the air. Pretty ingenious but it may not be that easy to invent. Well in the meantime maybe I will consider buying some property about ten miles from the beach and just wait a few years until I own beach front property. Of course I might have to sell quickly, if you know what I mean.

Paperless Society

I have worked for many companies during my occupation on this earth, and I noticed recently that most companies have a goal to be paperless if you will. I think with the onset of the computer age this was a realization of many corporations and smaller companies. But you know what? I don't think it will ever happen, that is going paperless. For one thing mankind has been writing things down for too long. Old habits are hard to break. For instance in the office where I work now, we have fancy copiers that scan, print and fax. All these features are really nice and convenient. If you consider what I just wrote though, you will notice I mentioned printing and faxing. Printing and faxing create a piece of paper, so even though we are getting more technologically advanced, we are still using paper. If we were truly a paperless society, there would not be a need for printing. Everything would be viewed from the computer screen. There would be no need for faxing, everything would be sent by email or scanned to email. A paperless society would be void of anything written on paper, including magazines, newspapers, bills, receipts, traffic tickets and the list goes on and on. If I wanted to read the newspaper on Saturday morning while I sit outside enjoying my coffee and cigarette, I would have to view it on line from my laptop computer. I just don't know if I could adjust to this new concept, I guess I am just old fashioned, as I am used to the shuffling of paper. Imagine you would not have to check your mailbox, because mail would be sent to you on line. Hey, does that mean no more junk mail? There would be no need for checkbooks because all payments to creditors would be sent on line. I guess that would be good for those who can't balance their checkbook because they would get an error message if they tried to pay for something on line but didn't have the funds in their account. So that would put an end to the so called "hot check". You know our society is littered with all the paper we don't want. Have you ever looked down at the roadside while you were sitting at a traffic light and noticed all the trash on the side of the road? God, I hope I'm not the only one that has ever done this. In any event you will notice discarded paper, cans, cigarette packages, wrappings from fast food and such. Let's face it, humans are trashy. In a paperless society there would not be as much litter on the roads. People who didn't win the lottery would not throw their unlucky lottery tickets out the window while they were driving down the road. I guess lottery tickets would be purchased on line and if you wanted to see if you won a million dollars you would go on line. Then the proceeds of your winning ticket would be deposited in your bank account through a wire transfer. Now there are some documents that could never be committed to a paperless means, such as your driver's license, social security card, birth certificate, marriage license, passport and other important documents. Or could they go paperless? Let's say you just got hired for a new job, and the employer asked for your social security card. In a paperless society, the employer would ask for your social security number instead. Now if you couldn't remember the number you would access your laptop computer or personal organizer to retrieve the number. Then you would verbally give the number to your employer, who would in turn access the number through a secured website. The website would find a match for the number given, which would identify you by name and date of birth. Perhaps the trend of the future will be a database that identifies every single human by name, date of birth and so on. It could also contain an updated picture for positive identification. Now what if you got stopped by a traffic cop? Normally the cop would ask you for your driver's license. In the paperless society you would give the cop your license number, again accessing the number from your P.C. or electronic organizer. The cop would in turn enter the number through the police computer, and your information would be displayed along with your picture ID. The cop would then enter your violation via the computer and come back to your vehicle to let you know you have received a citation and the citation will be emailed to you within twenty four hours. Wow, this really plays with my head. Somehow getting a citation on line doesn't seem as stressful. All these transactions seem sort of like science fiction, but I can almost visualize a paperless society within say twenty years from now. However there are a couple of obstacles to think about such as satellite disruption, power failures and electrical storms. Remember the Y2K event from the year 2000? Everyone was ready for modern society to crash and burn, but it never happened. In the meantime I guess I'm glad we are not a paperless society. There is something about turning the page of a magazine that I enjoy. Maybe it is the feel of the slick page with all the colorful images, or the sound of the pages rustling in the wind while I am sitting outside. Or the feeling of empowerment while I cut out the money saving coupons from the newspaper, knowing I will be in charge of my financial fate as I save money on my next grocery bill. Whatever happens I'm sure our society will become more dependent on the computer, and I think it will be good in most respects. On second thought, I think our society is already at that point, it is just a matter of implementing all the processes I described. Perhaps we could be that futuristic generation that many futurists only dreamed of. I think it will be interesting to see how our high tech future evolves.

Recycling for our Future

Let's face it humans are trashy, as I mentioned before. Did you ever stop to consider how much trash you accumulate in one day? It is mind boggling. Everyday when I get to work, my trash can is empty. By the end of the day is full of papers, plastic bags from my lunch, my empty cigarette packages and more. At home it's even worse. After preparing dinner each night, there are empty cans, empty two litter bottles, empty plastic containers from the margarine, dip, or whatever. We really do live in a packaged society. This results in tons and tons of trash everyday. I remember when my first son was born in the mid 1970's, I used cloth diapers. Yes it is true. By the time my daughter was born in the late 1970's, I used cloth and disposable diapers, depending on the money situation. Nowadays I'll bet moms don't even know how to use cloth diapers. This is just one example of how our society depends on packaged goods. Now when you throw your trash away at home, wherever you live, it goes in the trash container or dumpster. Then it goes to the dump. Most people don't take the time to recycle because they're too busy, too lazy, or just don't care. That's fine, sometimes I am lazy too. But what if our trash bags were modified to make it easy to recycle? You see, it goes back to my sorting obsession. Imagine it is Wednesday night, after preparing dinner you have all that trash to discard. I suggest the trash bags or liners be modified so there are two parts. One part would be for recycled goods such as plastic containers, plastic bags, cans, glass bottles, paper and cardboard. The other part would be for other garbage. Now here's the best part, if the manufacturer could make the bag perforated, you would have one bag with two sections, but when you remove the bag from the trash can, you could tear the two sections apart, and voila, you have a separate bag for your recycled trash and another for regular garbage. It would also be great if the manufacturer could make the bags or liners "colored" to make your job easier. I would suggest green for the recyclable trash and brown or white for the other garbage. It so ingenious that anyone could recycle. And when the trash bag is full, simply separate the two sections and let the waste management company do the rest.

We could all be recycling Kings and Queens. And this would set a precedent for our children as they observe their parents recycling at home. Hopefully it would instill the same mindset for them as they grow older. I'm sure some people wouldn't follow the rules, but if most us did, we could make use of recycled goods and save our valuable resources. I remember when I was a young girl my parents had one of those silver metal trash cans. It used to be so noisy when the trash collector picked it up. They would throw it down, or set it down hard, and sometimes the lid would fall off. It was a noisy neighborhood on trash day. And if you bought a new shiny trash can, it would look good for a couple of months. Then it would get bent out of shape from all the abuse from the trash collector, and the bright silvery paint would eventually tarnish, and became a dull grey. Then they came out with plastic containers that we are familiar with today. I don't think it really matters what the containers look like, they're all pretty ugly. Now back to the office where paper is wasted on a huge scale. You know the fax confirmation page that prints out whenever you send a fax? I'll bet they go in the trash but they shouldn't. I reuse mine for scratch paper. You could also save a box at a time and donate the paper to a church or school. Or save the paper to be recycled. It is really sickening when I think about how much waste is not recycled. Though I am not the Queen of recycling, I just think we as a society could do more. One more suggestion, there should be a receptacle for junk mail at the site of those centralized mailboxes, you know where there are a bunch of mailboxes in your neighborhood or apartment complex. This should be implemented by the U.S. Post Office. The junk mail receptacle would be secured so no one could steal the mail. Then the post office would return the unwanted junk mail to a place where it could be recycled. You see, it just takes a little thought and effort to make our world a cleaner and less wasteful place. Oh, and don't forget about the paper in your shredder, it can be recycled too. Recycling just takes a little thought and planning. And it would help if there were more recycling stations available in major cities. I think part of the problem is that many people don't know what to do with their recycled goods and they end up throwing them away. What if the local grocer offered a recycling station? I believe people's mindset would change because they would have a convenient way to recycle on a regular basis as most people go grocery shopping weekly. Maybe schools, churches and other community organizations need to offer incentives to recycle. If retailers could get involved also that would be great. With a combined effort our future could be cleaner and more cost efficient, definitely a win, win situation for the planet.

Let's Wake Up and Get Rid of Daylight Savings Time

I had to write about this subject because it is so bothersome to me. This has to be one of the most ridiculous endeavors our government has ever implemented. "Daylight Savings Time" or "DST" went into effect in the early 1900's. That should give one a clue that this law is outdated. The actual date was March 19th, 1918. If I made a list of things I could do without, it would consist of TV commercials, non-smoking restaurants, telephone solicitors, and yes you guessed it, Daylight Savings Time. I don't know all the reasoning and politics behind the time change, and I don't want to. I just know it is an inconvenience. I especially hate changing the clocks in the fall time. I get used to driving to work in the dark, and then the time change happens. The following Monday I notice a bright, glaring object in the eastern sky as the sun makes its untimely arrival. I have to fumble for my sunglasses, but my sunglasses are only useful when I'm driving eastward. When I turn the street corner and head north it's still dark, so I have to remove my sunglasses. It's all very annoying. And then there's the disruption of having to change all the clocks forward or backwards. Fortunately I own one of those atomic clocks, which automatically sets the time. What a great invention, but what about all the other clocks? There's the alarm clock, the clock on the stove and microwave, the clock in your automobile, the time clock at work, my wristwatch and the list goes on. I especially hate changing the clock in my vehicle because I always have to get out the owners manual. It's really hard to drive, read the owners manual, and figure out which buttons to push all at the same time. You push one of the buttons while you're at the red light, then the light turns green. By the time you get to the next red light, you have to start over. Well you are probably saying, "been there, done that". Here's another scenario, one gets to work, punches in on the time clock, and the wrong times shows on their time card, so it looks like they were an hour late. I believe we should not tamper with time. What difference does it make if the sun rises or sets an hour earlier? Humans can adjust to the natural rhythm of the sun and earth. Supposedly we humans had no problem adjusting for thousands of years, so why ruin a good thing? I suggest we make one final time change by moving the clock one hour forward or backwards, it doesn't matter to me, and leave it alone for prosperity. Oh, one thing I almost forget. There is one state which does not adhere to the time change. It is Arizona. Now imagine how screwed up that is if you live in say New Mexico and travel to Arizona on a regular basis. You would probably feel like you're in a time warp, having to constantly figure out the real time. And what about the cost associated with the time change? Someone has to pay for all the advertising to remind us of the time change, and though it may seem menial, it is your tax dollars being spent. I hope some politicians will get on the ball and get rid of this nuisance once and for all. I did take notice that in 2007 the time change was delayed about a month, so maybe there is a plan in the works that our government isn't telling us about. Well I hope so and I'm sure our grandchildren and great-grandchildren will appreciate the gesture. But I will still keep my atomic clock, it is awesome. But really, let's ask our government officials to get rid of the time change once and for all.

Doomsday (Coming to a Town near You)

Wherever you live in America, there is probably some threat of natural or unnatural disaster. Be it earthquakes, hurricanes, tornadoes or snowstorms we're all at the mercy of Mother Nature. A few summers ago in the Houston-Galveston area we were threatened by Hurricane Rita. Fortunately the storm barely missed us and we were spared.

However, it still affected a large number of us because some dumb ass gave a mass evacuation order for the whole population of Houston, Galveston and the surrounding areas. Now grant it the storm could have hit us and no one knew that in advance. First of all I should give you a quick geography lesson about the Houston-Galveston area. Galveston is an island city south of Houston which is connected by one major bridge. Galveston and many of the areas south of Houston are exposed to the Gulf of Mexico. These are low lying areas that are subject to flooding and storm surges as there are many bays and inlets that empty into the Gulf of Mexico. Houston is approximately fifty miles north of Galveston. Now I could understand evacuating Galveston and the areas close to the Gulf of Mexico, but not the city of Houston because it is pretty far inland. Do you have any idea what it's like to have millions of crazy people on the freeway all at the same time? I say crazy because these evacuees, if you will, are confused, panicked and at their wits end. And they're all going the same direction! Then add in the fact that the gas stations ran out of gas. I guess the people that planned the evacuation order didn't think about the gas situation. So now you have people who are stranded on the freeway because they ran out of gas, and they are confused, panicked and blocking the freeway lanes. Oh, and did I mention the temperature was in the upper nineties with high humidity? This happened in the month of September which is very hot in Houston. Many people couldn't run their AC in their vehicles because they were low on gas, and this caused many people to run out of patience. My mind is wandering again as I remember those old monster movies I used to watch on Saturday mornings where Godzilla, a fictional Japanese monster, was coming down the road, and all the people were running and screaming as the monster got closer. I remember the look on their faces as they tried to run but they knew the monster was gaining on them. Then someone in the crowd would turn their head around once in awhile to see where the monster was and they became more terrified as they realized the monster was right behind them. There was always someone who tripped and fell down, and their fate was doomed. Oh yea, I remember the comparison now. Anyways, all the evacuees are driving instead of running, but they're not getting anywhere because the average speed was about three miles per hour. My daughter and my two youngest sons were among the evacuees. They decided to go to their grandparent's lake house located northeast of Houston. It is normally less than a two hour drive from Houston but if I remember correctly it took around sixteen hours to reach their destination. My daughter had her gas sucking SUV loaded up with food, clothing, important papers, family pictures and the family dog. Now here's the real irony, once my daughter and two younger sons reached their grandparents house I'm sure they were probably relieved and maybe a little irritable after being in the vehicle for sixteen hours. As it turns out Hurricane Rita was following them as they ended up right in the path of the storm. Talk about a worried mom. Yes the storm made landfall east of the Houston-Galveston area and made its path towards east Texas and Louisiana. Now there is a lesson to be learned from all this. First of all the authorities need to rethink the evacuation plan. I believe it should be done in stages, and that the roadways should be cleared of all inbound traffic. They also need to make sure that there is plenty of gasoline available because in a crisis situation everyone wants to fill up with gas. I don't know how they could do it, but perhaps bring gasoline in from other cities before they give the evacuation orders. Secondly they could divide the evacuation routes by using color codes for the vehicles. For instance anyone who drives a white, green or red vehicle would have to use one route, and anyone driving a black, silver or brown vehicle would use a different route. This way everyone would not be using the same evacuation route. Another idea would be to set up help stations along the routes for people who might need water, mechanical assistance for their vehicles or medical aid. You know when all is said and done, I believe this was a good rehearsal for our town. All major cities need to look at their plans and maybe compare plans with other cities. Who would have known that Hurricane Ike was going to make Houston its bulls-eye when it reached the shores of Galveston in September 2008? Its devastation was not so much in the loss of lives, but rather property damage and several thousand homes were without electricity for weeks. While hurricanes are somewhat predictable, earthquakes and other disasters are not predictable. Every city needs to have assigned shelters, evacuation routes and emergency services in place. They should also have a group of volunteer citizens on call for providing other services. Now in the event of say a nuclear war, if you survive, you're pretty much on your own. But for other disasters my husband came up with a good idea for a meeting place for our family members. I believe if you have family members that don't live with you a meeting place should be set forth in case of an emergency and communications are down. He said the best place to meet everyone would be the cemetery where my Mom and Dad are laid to rest. While that may seem a little strange, it really is a good idea because in the event of a disaster who would be in a hurry to get to a cemetery? It is really up to each individual to be prepared. I thought it would be a good idea to fill an ice chest or one of those plastic coolers with some necessities and put it away in a closet or some place accessible in the event of a disaster. Some of the items one could put away are canned goods, (don't forget the can opener), MRE's (meals ready to eat), a medical kit, blankets, important phone numbers, a map, a flashlight with extra batteries and maybe a weapon for self defense. Oh, and don't forget cash. One more thing you could do is prepare a list of other items that you would need to grab before you go, such as prescription drugs, diapers, important papers, food for your animals, ammo and whatever else is important. Put the check list on top of all the other stuff so you can grab it quickly. Now you are somewhat prepared in case of an emergency, or at the very least if you run out of cash or groceries, you have some stashed away. The same philosophy could be applied to the family vehicle. You should always have a few items put away in case you are stranded such as a flashlight, a blanket, some bottled water, basic tools and battery jumper cables. I guess most people think nothing bad will happen to them. I hope nothing bad does happen, but I would rather be prepared. And last but not least, know which roads you would use if you had to evacuate. And remember our family meeting place I mentioned earlier? It is a good idea to discuss a meeting place with your family members in advance. Name a place that everyone is familiar with and knows how to get to, like the local skating rink, the baseball field or the church. It just takes a little bit of time and effort to plan ahead, but it could the best insurance you have in case doomsday comes to your town.

Working and Living, We Will Survive

Sometimes we get so caught up trying to make it through the day we miss all the little things, like the aroma of that first cup of coffee, our children's smiles as they leave for school, the neighbor waving as we leave for work, the beautiful sunset that reminds us of God's perfect world and the list could go on and on. Unfortunately life is not perfect, so we shall see, but it never hurts to dream.

The New Job Application

No matter who you are, you have probably filled out a job application sometime in your life. This can be a very daunting task. You put on your best clothes, fix your hair and do a double take in the mirror before you head out. You're probably already depressed because you don't have a job, or maybe you're thinking of changing jobs and you're depressed about your current job. You drive to the new company, park, and sit in your car a few moments to compose yourself. You feel nervous but you're already there so you get out of the car and go inside. You approach the front desk with a sense of false security and an awkward smile as you introduce yourself to the receptionist. Then you are handed the "application". You sit down and with pen in hand began filling out the application. The application is redundant as you are asked you where you were employed twenty years ago, how long you have lived at your current residence, how long you lived at your previous residence, and so on. You are also asked for your social security number, past job information, job skills, and personal information such as your race, gender and any criminal background. I think it is ridiculous. I think all companies should recycle all those stupid applications and start over. First of all the potential employer doesn't need our whole life history. All they need to know is our name, address, phone number and what skills one possesses. They don't need our personal information unless we are considered for the job. Let's face it, they are not going to do a background check or check references unless they plan to hire the person being considered. So why must we indulge all our personal and other irrelevant information? I believe a standard for the new job application would be a basic one page application that would look something like this:

What position are you applying for?
First Name and last Name:
Current Residence: (no P.O. boxes please):
Phone number:
Alternate phone number:
Email Address:
Current or Previous Employer:
Address and phone number of current or previous employer:
How long at the current or previous job:
List five skills that qualify you for the position you are applying for:

At the end of the application the employer could put the following stipulation:

If you are considered for employment, we will request a copy of your driver's license and social security card. In addition a background check and/or drug test may be required. Thank you for your interest and you will be notified if you are considered for employment.

I believe this new and generic job application should go into force as it provides enough information for the employer. The new application would only take a few minutes to complete and let's face it the employer is only going to look at a couple of things, your skills, and your past employment. A company doesn't really need to know where I've been employed for the last twenty years. For God's sake, what if the person applying for the job is only twenty five years old? They're not going to have twenty years of employment history to record but they may be a good candidate for the job. Nowadays almost everyone has a resume prepared so the job application is redundant to say the least. Because when it comes down to it you're either qualified or you're not qualified. And there's one question I especially hate, which is "do you have dependable transportation?" What difference does it make how one gets to work as long as they get there? Now grant it depending on the job, the employer may need to know certain information if it relates to the job, such as can you lift heavy loads, for say a warehouse job. But the company I am applying with doesn't need to know about my hobbies or outside interests. What if I respond by writing I enjoy target shooting on the weekends as my hobby. Is that response going to affect my chances of getting hired even though I am being honest? I just feel that the whole process could be simplified and made a little less frustrating for everyone concerned. And by the way, I'd like to know what happens to all those job applications from people who don't get hired? Just another good reason why our personal information should never be given out until it is necessary. All a company needs to know about me is one thing, am I qualified to do the job? They don't need to know about my hobbies, religious preference, how many children I have, my marital status, if I'm male or female, or something in between, or what color my skin is. Something you should think about the next time you fill out that ridiculous four page job application. And by the way, good luck.

Labor Day Weekend

It is Friday and I am at my office early again. I have starred at the white page in front of me long enough. Perhaps I am having difficulty writing because I am thinking about the three day weekend for Labor Day. I don't know who started the tradition of "Labor Day"; I suppose it is one of those stupid holidays to honor people who work. That's alright with me, I'll take it. I suppose I should be caught up in the frenzy of excitement but my husband has already mentioned his plans for the weekend. He has to get new tires for the truck which translates into washing the truck afterwards. The car also needs to be washed, the house needs to be cleaned, the grocery shopping done and so I will be laboring on the Labor Day weekend. I suppose I should count my blessings though because things could always be worse. I could be unemployed or too sick to work. I am fortunate that I have a decent job with employers who treat me well and pay me a fair salary. I think I am rather lucky. Now there are those who love to complain at the workplace and no matter how great their job is they will constantly complain. These people are unhappy souls. They spend their time analyzing people and situations that give them reasons to complain. They complain about the weather, they complain about the temperature inside in the building, it's always too hot or too cold, they complain about their computers not working fast enough. They complain about the food they eat, the clothes they wear, the car they drive, their co-workers and generally anything they can complain about. These people need counseling because they do not know how to find happiness. I feel sorry for anyone who is in a relationship with a "complainer" because all that negative energy has to go somewhere. If I had to counsel someone who was a "complainer" my first instruction would be for them to write down five good things about their life in general. For example I woke up this morning, which is a good thing. I got to my job without incident which is a good thing. I had a fresh cup of coffee which is more than some people have in the morning. I experienced a good night's sleep in a comfortable and warm bed next to the man I love. Many people sleep on the streets and have no one to comfort them. I had the opportunity and inspiration to write my book while many people do not have the education or means to write or explore their creativity. Now I would like to put things in perspective. Everyone complains about something from time to time. The whole essence of my book is basically complaining about society. But there's a difference between complaining and doing nothing and complaining while trying to resolve the situation at hand. At the workplace we are forced to work among individuals we did not choose to relate to. We are thrown into the pot so to speak with a mix of employees we must work with rather we like it or not. Therefore we must try to get along the best we can. Chances are most people spend more awake hours at their job than they spend at home with their families. If you work and know someone who is a complainer try to use reverse psychology on them by being positive, complimentary and happy. You may be surprised at the results. But if all your positive energy does nothing to influence that person then stray from them before their negative energy affects you. Remember the purpose of working is to collect that paycheck at the end of the week. If you do a good job you can collect your payment in good faith. As for your co-workers, don't worry about their fate, they are not your responsibility. The only person you have to be accountable for is yourself. So what if your co-workers are lazy, hypochondriacs, or ass kissers? If the employer can accept these traits then you must also accept them. Unless the situation at your job becomes violent or criminal there is basically no recourse so you might as well deal with it. Remember work is one of those four letter words. We must work to make a living so I say "work and be happy".

A Man's World

My husband always tells me that men are responsible for building mostly everything we see in the world. He points this out when he sees construction workers building a house or new office building. He says, "Where are all the women?" as he refers to the workers. And I simply reply, "I don't know", because there are usually no women in sight. He makes his point time and time again, as we watch TV. Perhaps we are watching a program that shows how the Egyptian pyramids were built, and the program shows a reenactment as the scantily clothed men move the heavy stones with ropes, slowly ascending up the pyramid. I already know what my husband is going to say, "Where are all the women?" And I already know I will ignore my husband's question. However, my husband may have a point. Men are the stronger species of the human race and they also have the minds for building things. Women on the other hand, are the weaker species. I mean physically weaker. Not matter how much a woman strives to be strong, she will never be as strong as a man physically because women's bodies do not have the same structure as men's bodies. Maybe women are weaker physically, but not mentally or emotionally. I think men and women compliment each other. Even the strongest, toughest guy needs nurturing sometimes. Remember, that tough guy was a little boy at one time and his mother probably cared for him in a sweet and comforting way. Then that little boy grew up into a man. I'm not saying that guys are not emotional and caring, it's just women are more nurturing. Now God forbid but what if the roles were reversed and women were the builders of the world? Well, I'm afraid the world would be a much different place. Women would think of easy ways to build, for instance there probably wouldn't be any skyscrapers. Women would probably build roads around the mountains, as opposed to through the mountains. There probably wouldn't be any sports cars, because women don't have the need for speed as their male counterparts do. There probably wouldn't be any thrill rides at the amusements parks, instead just a few simple rides and maybe some beautiful gardens to enjoy. God help us because we probably wouldn't have microwave ovens, plastic, or computers. Now when one thinks of plastic, which half of the world is made of, one must understand that plastic is derived from oil. Could you envision a woman exploring for oil or creating the refineries needed to refine oil? Somehow it just doesn't seem likely. Now imagine a world without oil, free of greenhouse gases, thus global warming would not be an issue perhaps. And here's the big one, have you ever heard of a woman who started a war? Yes, I'm sure that in the past women did initiate battles or wars, but it was rare. If women were in charge, there would probably be a lot of bickering and gossip, but few wars to speak of. And women probably wouldn't have created weapons of mass destruction as men have created. I'm not suggesting that women are not capable of building or inventing great things. I'm sure there are women with the intellect and desire to do so. In the past women have made some great contributions to our world, but for the most part men have built the world around us and most of the technology we know. I guess I am thankful that men are in charge of our world. I will remember my words the next time I am sitting in traffic and listening to my satellite radio or watching the horrors of war on my big screen TV in my air conditioned house. Thanks guys

TGIF

Yes, thank God it's Friday! We work and toil for five days and Friday's are our reward, sort of the fruit of our labor. Of course there are those unfortunate souls they can't relate to the "thank God it's Friday" scenario such as those who work in hospitals, retail, restaurants etc…I feel pity for those unfortunate souls. But for the rest of us something magical begins to happen on Fridays. We laugh, smile and frolic at the workplace while we anticipate the day's end. We anxiously watch the clock as it nears 5:00 pm. We simulate work but there is really no work to be done past the lunch hour on Friday. Our one track mentality can only imagine the weekend, which is just beyond the threshold of the door at our workplace. Once that threshold is crossed we are no longer enslaved by our employers, but rather we are free for one weekend to do as we please. We can sleep late in the morning and leisurely arise from bed, wearing our bedtime attire as long as we like. We can stroll around our home with no purpose other than to stroll around. We can watch endless hours of television without worrying about sleep. We can go shopping and spend the hard earned money we made during the week. We can become silly and drunken without fear of being fired by anyone. We can take as many breaks as we like, sipping on cool drinks and puffing on cigarettes, while reading the whole newspaper. We can take a nap during the middle of the day. We can reunite with our families or neighbors who we have lost touch with during the week. As I imagine all these things I am interrupted by something as trivial as a phone call. I am at work and the time is 4:50 pm. My purse and car keys are in their position on my desk as a soldier would have their battle weapons ready for battle. I pretend to be working as I shuffle papers around, but keep a constant vigil on the clock. When I realize the phone is ringing I just look at it in disbelief. My senses become heightened as I check for any bosses that might be in the vicinity. Do I answer the phone or pretend I am not at my desk? I rationalize that if I do not answer the phone someone will page me overhead and my name will be heard by everyone in the office including the bosses. I reluctantly pick up the phone receiver and hear someone talking. I am oblivious to the words they utter as my eyes are drawn to my purse and keys again. Then a sudden moment of reality sinks in and I enter the phone conversation. Who could commit this sacrilegious act of calling at 4:50 pm on Friday? I continue the conversation and confess to the caller that I am fixing to leave and try to end the annoying conversation. As I hang up the receiver I wonder what could have been so important to the caller that they could not have waited until Monday morning to call. Perhaps they are not enticed by the weekend like I am, perhaps they do not have anything to look forward to, or perhaps they have to work on Saturday, which is the ultimate punishment for the weekender's cult. Now the time is 4:58 pm. This is the time I normally leave on Fridays but the phone call I received has delayed me. I close down my computer, grab my purse and keys and head straight for the door. No one can stop me now as I cannot see or hear my coworkers. As the light penetrating from the door becomes brighter I know I am almost free. Finally I am at the doorway and have reached the point of no return, well until Monday morning that is. As I walk out the door and breathe the outside air a feeling of freedom overcomes me. I look at the sun and the trees with a fresh new outlook on life. The weekend is finally here. Thank God.

Leisure Time, that's what I Need

Today I am writing while at my office in the early morning hours. It is stormy outside and occasionally I look out the window at the rain and lightning. I feel secure though as my office is small and cozy. I have been starring at my computer for awhile now, and realized I can't think of anything to write about. This is not good for a writer. I keep thinking about other things going on in my life such as my son who is trying to find a job, my husband who has been a little too spend thrifty lately, my eye appointment this Saturday, all my little aches and pains, the work that's piling up on my desk. All these distractions have created a fog in my mind that is concealing the words I need to write. Writing is not as easy as you may think. First you have to think of a topic that is interesting. Many times I think of things to write about while I am doing other things, like driving, working, talking on the phone or watching television. The problem is I soon forget these topics because I don't write down my thoughts at that particular time. So my thoughts fade away because I'm sometimes forgetful. Yes I admit it, that's part of the ageing process and I become more and more forgetful each day. And I just don't have enough leisure time. What I mean by leisure time is time to spend doing whatever I want to do. Unfortunately, there is little time to do what I want to do. Most of the time I do what my employers want me to do, or my husband wants me to do, or I am resting or relaxing from all the things I did for everyone else but me. It's really a miracle I even have time to write because there are few windows of opportunity to write with my busy schedule. One of those times is the early morning hours because there is no one around to make demands of me. I think I will get a refill of coffee, which may help me think of some ideas to write about. Darn, now I need to smoke a cigarette, one can't have a fresh cup of morning coffee without a cigarette. I'm back and I feel better now. Now I'm starting to become more focused. I was thinking about that leisure time I need while I was outside smoking and observing the passing storm. My idea of leisure time would be sitting at the picnic table outside on my patio with something cold to drink and a cigarette of course. The only sounds I would hear would be the songs from the birds, the neighbor's dog barking, an occasional car driving by and the whisper of the wind. With pen in hand I know I could write about many things. I wouldn't answer the phone or turn on the television. I would ignore my neighbor's distant conversations and the sounds of the children playing in the street. You see this is real leisure time. I don't need a tropical paradise, or a cruise ship full of strangers wearing shorts and sunglasses, or a plane ticket to some place I've never been, I just need the solitude of my backyard. My husband has been trying to plan a vacation for us and now I'm starting to imagine a vacation at home. Wouldn't that be nice? But I don't think my husband would agree because he wants to go boating. So again I am subjected to my husband wishes. But I'm sure if we go on vacation it will be worthwhile just to get away. So I guess I could force myself to go have fun in the sun and ride on the boat all day. After all one must make sacrifices sometimes. On the other hand if I was to use all the money my husband would spend on our vacation to experience a vacation at home, I could buy a shit load of beer and cigarettes and have money left over. We could buy some items to fix up the house, or go to the movie theatre as often as we like. We could dine out everyday because I sure as hell wouldn't feel like cooking. We could stay up late at night and sleep late in the morning while our neighbors leave for work. I would turn the alarm clock off and hope I remembered to turn it back on when the vacation was over. I could organize all my family pictures and put them in new picture frames. I could take one of those candlelit bubble baths like the ladies in the magazine. Man all this is starting to sound good. I think I will try to convince my husband to take a vacation at home. Now all the leisure time sounds wonderful but I should be thankful that I have a job and that I'm able to take a vacation. I should also be thankful for all my family that keeps me occupied, because without them life would be very lonely. So I may not be a lady of leisure, but I can always dream, dream of leisurely, lazy afternoons. That is something I no one can take away from me.

I Can't Take It Anymore!

We as a society are bombarded with advertising. No matter where one goes there is no refuge. Even in the privacy of our own home, or especially in our home, television and internet ads continually assault us. Well I know as long as there is commercialism we will never be able to escape the onslaught, but maybe there should be some changes made, for our sanity of course.

Those Darned TV Commercials

Simply put I am so sick of all the inappropriate advertising on TV. When I say "inappropriate" I am referring to the ads aimed at adults and their intimate problems. Why do these commercials bombard us right around dinnertime? The pharmaceutical companies must be making millions of dollars if they can afford to air their commercials during prime time television, which is when I'm usually watching the news or my favorite television programs after a long day of work at the office. A few years ago I didn't know what EDS meant, but now I do. I'm sure by now everyone knows that EDS stands for "erectile dysfunction syndrome". I think these commercials are inappropriate for prime time television. That also includes commercials related to sexual enhancement drugs, sanitary products and, well you get the picture. I'm sick of seeing those commercials of middle aged men walking around with those stupid smiles on their faces. Or the commercial with the man and woman in the bathtub situated in a nature setting. For God sakes please give me a break. I really don't think these commercials are appropriate for younger audiences to watch. It's not so much the content of these commercials that bothers me, but rather the fact that they are shown during prime time television. I believe these commercials need their own time slot which is not during prime time television. If you think your children don't pay attention to these commercials you might be surprised. Children can be very observant and much more sensitive than we imagine. These types of commercials are aimed at adults, and should be shown at appropriate times. Now I know the pharmaceuticals companies are raking in the money because the cost of prescription drugs here in America is obscene. As a result the pharmaceutical companies can afford to advertise whenever and wherever they want. Mind you the cost for those same prescription drugs in other countries is a lot less or no cost at all for countries that have universal health care. You probably already know this if you have ever watched "60 Minutes" or any other news hour programming about socialized or universal health care. But not in America where the pharmaceutical companies have the freedom to charge whatever they want and get away with it. And there's nothing we can do about it. As a result we are subjected to their commercialism for whatever ails us Americans. I think the television producers need to evaluate the content of any commercial and ask if it's appropriate for children to watch. If not the commercials should only be shown before or after the prime time slot. I know this would make the pharmaceutical companies mad, but that's too damned bad. I would consider anytime from 7:00 am to 9:00 pm prime time and that time slot should apply to all television stations including the cable television stations. Basically if it is awkward to explain to your twelve year old what the commercial is advertising, then it should not be shown during prime time hours. Somehow when I sit down in my cozy recliner to eat dinner and watch the 6:00 news I get a bad taste in my mouth when I see those stupid couples trying to find the optimum time to get it on. I really don't care about his defects and the drug that last for thirty six hours. Now the pharmaceutical companies might think they have won because if I'm writing about their commercials they've obviously made an impact on me. You know they might be right but all I am saying is be selective about the time the commercials are shown. Oh, one last thing. For God sakes stop showing the same commercials over and over. There should be a shelf life for each commercial, say ninety days. Because that's just about how long I can tolerate watching the same commercial, over and over, like a bad dream. If I remember correctly when cable TV was first introduced, it was commercial free. Whatever happened to that concept? Well the cable companies got greedy, that's what happened. I understand we can't avoid the annoying commercials, but perhaps the television stations could be more selective about what commercials are shown during prime time. By the way, what ever happened to that Marlboro man that used ride his horse off into the sunset? Now that was a good commercial.

Signs of the Times

While I'm on the subject of advertising, I thought I would get it all out of my system. We as a society are subjected to commercials on television, radio, and our computers. You think one would find sanctuary in their automobile but even a short drive yields more advertising. We just can't escape it. When you drive your car through that vast concrete jungle you are subjected to advertising the minute you exit the neighborhood wherever you live. I'm talking about those annoying billboard signs that are strategically placed next to the road wherever you drive. You're trying to concentrate on your driving and there it is; a mega billboard sign with a picture of an oversized man or woman starring down at you, their inappropriate size seems sort of eerie. You may see a woman who is scantily clothed looking directly at you as if she was inviting you to have a drink with her. Or you may see an attractive businessman with a perfect smile trying to sell you insurance. Another billboard sign displays the state lottery numbers for the last lottery with the huge winning numbers posted so you can't miss them. Hell I already knew I didn't win the lottery but I still have to try and memorize the numbers real quick before

I pass the sign. Imagine you notice a billboard sign that is worthy of your glance, all of a sudden as you drive past the sign you realize you are much closer to the car in front of you and you brake just in time. You have been distracted looking at a stupid billboard sign that appeared from nowhere but managed to steal your attention for a few critical seconds while you were driving. It is like a frenzy of signs competing for your attention, one placed right after another with huge letters and vivid colors. Then you approach the light at the intersection and you may or may not notice those stupid homemade cardboard signs cluttering the street corners. Shouldn't it be illegal to post signs on government property such as light poles or traffic signs? There are signs of all sizes and shapes, weathered and worn from the elements, trying to get your attention with their deceptive messages. I see it all the time, "3 bedroom house for rent", "loose weight fast", "landscaping services", "we remodel anything", "we can fix your credit" (yeah right), and the list goes on. Those who advertise on the street corners by taping their homemade signs to the street sign or lamp poles should be stopped. The companies they represent are what I call "fly by night" companies. They can't afford the regular means of advertising so they clutter the intersections of America with their desperate ads. The signs are usually taped or stapled in a hastily manner in hopes that some sucker will actually write down the phone number. First of all it doesn't look nice and when the signs fall off they litter the roadways. So why don't the police remove the signs and then call the telephone numbers so they can fine the solicitors? It's simple to remedy. Simply find out whose name the phone number is listed to and ticket that person for the displaying an illegal sign. Well as I mentioned before it should be illegal but I guess it depends on the local jurisdiction. Now I know companies want to advertise and they should have a right to do so. But advertising on the roadways is not the answer. There should be other means of advertising that don't distract people who are driving. And that is the point I am trying to stress. The shopping malls would be a good place to advertise. You already have people who are in "spending money mode" at the mall, and they can read the signs while they walk around. Public bathrooms are a good place to advertise as you have a fixed audience while they take care of their business. I know a really good place to advertise for weight loss drugs or exercise clubs, the dressing rooms at clothing stores. When people find out they can't fit into the clothes they want to buy perhaps they will consider the advertising for those ads. Believe me, there is nothing as scrutinizing as the mirror in the dressing room. Want to advertise for children's products? Advertise in the public school system or at day care centers. Those institutions could probably use the proceeds from the advertising. Now I see a lot of advertising displayed on vehicles as well. Companies try to be creative by displaying pictures and ads on their vehicles. There is no way you could read all the information while you're driving and besides it is distracting. Now here is my solution to advertising on vehicles. Advertising should only be displayed on the backside of the vehicle. This way one who is passing or driving next to the vehicle will not be distracted. If one is behind the vehicle that is advertising their driving is less inhibited. Of course that means that public and private vehicles would have to remove any advertising on the sides of their vehicles. I would hope for the passage of a "clean advertising act" if you will. This act would cause the elimination of all billboard or roadside advertising. We would have a less cluttered society with cleaner streets and roadways. Plus it would be nice to drive somewhere and notice the trees and sky without billboards signs blocking my view. Mind you advertising will never go away and I probably don't want it to because sometimes I do discover products that deserve my attention. I just feel that outside advertising should be restricted or removed. We have enough distractions in life and besides we need to concentrate on our driving because someone has to be watching out for all the idiots driving around out there.

The Shadow People

I refer to them as the "shadow people" because these people remind me of a scary dream, someone is lurking the in the shadows but I never know who they are or what they're going to do to me, but I know it's not good. The "shadow people" I am referring to are the predators who want to steal from you and me. They have no conscious or morals. We've all heard about it and some of us unfortunate souls have experienced it. Imagine, your life is going along good, then you get your credit card or bank statement, and a dark cloud descends upon your horizon of normalcy. You don't recognize the charges, or discover that your bank account has been wiped out, and you wonder how did this happen. I remember when my Mom got her first credit card. It was a revolving charge card, whatever that meant. Back in those days, people referred to credit cards as "charge cards". Now our society is overwhelmed with credit cards, debit cards and on line banking and bill paying. I must receive at least two or three credit card offers in the mail almost daily. It is sickening and such a waste of paper. But on the other end of the spectrum, there are those of us who would like to receive a credit card offer, but no longer do because someone took advantage of them, and now their credit is ruined. Part of the problem is stolen credit card accounts and I think I know a way to prevent this, or at least partially prevent it. Whenever I receive my credit card statement, that dreadful time of month, I notice that my account number is referenced several times on the statement. Why is this necessary? I suggest that the credit card companies only reference part of the account number. I have seen statements that reference only the last four digits, and show the account number as follows: Your account ending in "9999". Why can't this be done across the board? Obviously we know it's our account if the statement shows up in our mailbox with our name on it. But in the event that someone else ends up with our statement guess what? They will not have access to the whole account number. I believe a national law should be passed that makes it illegal to reference any bank, credit card or retail account number in whole. The lender would only be able to reference a portion of the account number. This would also apply to social security numbers and banking account numbers. If the national law I spoke if earlier went into effect creditors and banks could use some type of bar code to scan the statements to recognize the whole account number. They could call the new law the "Consumer Account Protection Act". This practice could also be implemented for on line services. You would simply enter part of your account number along with a password. I also thought about using PIN numbers whenever doing a credit or debit card transaction. I already have a PIN number associated with my bank account, but what about using a PIN number with credit and debit card accounts? The cardholder would be asked to select a PIN number when they open an account. When you swipe your card to pay for something the machine would ask for your PIN number to complete the transaction. This would prevent anyone from being able to use your stolen credit or debit card because they wouldn't know your PIN number. Grant it having a PIN number for every account could be confusing, especially if you forget the number. So I suggest using the same PIN number for all your accounts and picking a number that is easy to remember. For instance you could pick a number that is easy to remember, such as the year you graduated from high school, the year you got married, or the year your firstborn child was born. But I would stray from using a number associated with your date of birth, social security number, or address. Because you just never know, someone could get lucky if they have access to that information. But most people are not going to know what year you graduated from high school. Believe me the criminals would still find some way to operate, but it would make their job much harder. I also suggest using a personal shredder. This inexpensive device could save you a lot of time, money and frustration. If you get in the habit of shredding all those credit card and bank statements, no one will ever be able to retrieve that information from your trash or dumpster. If you don't have a personal shredder, you can tear off the account numbers before you discard your statements. Your personal account numbers are your lifeline to doing business in our commercialized society. Never, ever give any personal information to anyone who calls you to solicit something. When my phone rings at home I always check the caller ID. If it is a number I don't recognize I usually do not answer the phone. But sometimes I am not paying attention and do answer the phone. As soon as I hear that unfamiliar and way too cheery voice on the phone asking me if I am the lady of the house, I hang up. I can do that because I have the power to do that. It is my house, my phone, and I pay the phone bill. Nowadays you cannot trust anyone. But if you're one of those people who have less resistance, and someone calls you to sell something you are interested in, ask the caller for their phone number so you can consider the offer and call them back. If it is someone who is trying to deceive you, they will not give you a phone number. If they are legitimate, they will. Chances are they will not offer you a phone number, instead they will argue with you by stating you must take advantage of the special offer immediately. These sub-humans are tenacious as they have mastered the art of persuasion and never take no for an answer. That is why it is best to hang up before they have a chance to infiltrate your defenses. It's really just common sense. These solicitors use tactics to pressure you such as "this is a limited time offer", or "I can only offer this price today", or "in order to be in our sweepstakes, you must order now". It's all BS! How many people do you know that have ever won a sweepstakes? I can predict that it is probably 0. Chances are there isn't a sweepstakes to begin with. So don't fall prey to this growing frenzy of deception. All they want is your money or to steal your personal credit information.

Personally I feel that telephone soliciting should be illegal. It never fails, I am at home, enjoying a restful evening watching TV or sitting outside on the patio, and the phone rings. I jump up to see who's calling and it is a long distance phone number I don't recognize, so I suspect it is another telephone solicitor. I wish I had a magic button on my phone that would send an electrical charge to the caller and give them a hell of a shock. Unfortunately my phone does not have that feature. Why doesn't our government pass a "No telephone soliciting law"? This law would prevent retailers from selling phone list with my name and phone number. It all comes down to staying aware and vigilant when protecting one's credit. I would suggest that one cannot be overly cautious, because you never know who is lurking in the shadows.

Just another Day

You know we go through life every day facing the same routines, but sometimes we encounter something out of the norm that makes us stop and wonder. I like little surprises and I believe everyday should have at least one surprise.

The Routine of Life

I know we are creatures of habit, everything in nature, including human behavior, is based on cycles. The sun rises, the humans wake up and go to work, the sun sets, we rest for another day. Most of the time this applies, but there are a few exceptions such as the night dwellers who are up at night when most of us are fast asleep. Some of these people have no choice as they work nighttime such as nurses, doctors, police and the people who work at the twenty four hour fast food restaurants, and I have to confess that hamburger at 2:00 am taste pretty good. Anyways, I never really paid attention to what the rest of the world was doing at 5:00 am until my husband and I started carpooling together. My husband's job required him to be at work at 5:30 am and when you only have one vehicle carpooling is the way to go. It all started with innocent conversation when I carpooled with my husband and he started pointing out certain vehicles he recognized on our daily commute to work. At first I thought my husband was weird as he would say "look, there's that black truck without the tailgate, watch, it will turn right at the next light", and I'll be damned if it didn't turn right at the next light. I know my husband is not a stalker, because we go almost everywhere together. However, he is one of the most observant people I know. So then I started to notice the trend of things too, we would pass certain vehicles almost daily that we'd seen before. I wondered if the people in those unsuspecting vehicles had observed us in the same way that my husband and I had observed them while they were innocently driving down the road. Somehow I doubt it. They probably just wanted to enjoy the peace and quite of their morning commute and sip on their coffee. My husband went on to explain how almost everyone pretty much follows the same routine. So I thought I would share my morning routine to see if there are others out there like me.

My morning starts early as my husband awakens me around 4:00am. I slowly arise to a semi-upright position as I sit up on the bedside pondering if I really want to get up. Then I rationalize that if I don't get up I will miss my ride to work, so I slowly stand up. After I experience the little aches and pains of midlife, I leave my bedroom sanctuary and move slowly towards the light, which would be the bathroom. I get a little break as I sit in a state of semi-consciousness taking care of my business. I might doze off a couple of seconds while I take care of my business, but who would know? Afterwards I head towards the vanity where I see my face start to come into focus in the mirror. I study my zombie like appearance, mumble "to hell with it", as I take a breath, and remember I am on a mission, or more realistically, that I only have twenty minutes left to get ready. I become robot like as I shower, brush my teeth and apply the wrinkle cream that probably doesn't work. I swipe on some eye shadow and lipstick for the finale. Now off to the closet to get dressed, but wait, I hear a familiar voice coming from the bedroom. It is my husband, who is the master of routine, yelling "are you ready yet"? He must have listened to the sounds of my bathroom activities and learned certain queues. This way he knew exactly when to ask me this trivial little question. If I was ready, I wouldn't be hanging out in the bathroom. When we were first married and I was more naïve, I would actually answered him with a "yea" or "I'm almost ready". But now I basically ignore all the voices coming from the bedroom early in the morning. Suddenly a dark, shadowy figure in the form of my husband appears at the bathroom door saying, "come on, it's time to go". Remember how I mentioned that my husband was the master of routine? You know how some people miss the boat? Well my husband would never miss the boat. In fact, he would probably be the captain of the boat, standing on the deck waiting to inspect all his mates. The only problem is he would think I was one of his mates. Let me explain. My husband wakes up about ten minutes before I do. I don't need an alarm clock because he is like clockwork. In twenty minutes he gets up, packs his lunch, does his bathroom routine, gets dressed and makes the bed. After the mad rush of getting ready he lies on the bed to gather a few minutes of rest while he waits for me to get ready. It's like he's in fast forward, while I'm standing in the closet wondering how I got there and trying to decide what I'm going to wear. It's really amazes me. Now do I wear the purple blouse with the black skirt again? Or the red blouse with the black pants? I don't think anyone really gives a shit, so I put on the black skirt with the purple blouse and prepare myself to face the world another day. On the way to work my husband makes small talk while I try to pretend I'm snoozing. Of course my husband does all the driving. It must be a macho thing as he hardly ever lets me drive. Now perhaps if it was WWIII it might be different. He might let me drive so he could shoot at someone to escape all the chaos, but even then he would be yelling at me with directions, such as turn there, drive faster, or don't slow down you dumb ass, something to that effect. Anyways, back to realty as I try to remember how I got ready so fast, it seems I was just standing in the closet. Oh, we're at my office now. My husband leans over to give me a quick kiss goodbye, and speeds off into the impending sunrise. Just another routine morning commute.

Cat Schmidt

My Pictures

Ever since I was young I always enjoyed looking at family pictures taken for whatever the occasion may have been. My mother used to keep the family pictures in the bottom of a dresser drawer. Whenever I got that warm fuzzy feeling to look at the pictures I would sit on the floor and gaze at the pictures for what seemed hours. In reality it was probably less time but I was so intrigued with the thought that whatever a person was doing, once their picture was taken, that event was frozen in time. Since there were six children in my family my parents didn't have a lot of time to take pictures. Therefore most of our family pictures were taken at events such as holidays and vacations. I can still remember Mom gathering all of us kids so my Dad could take a picture. Mom would fuss with our hair, tell us to stand up straight and make sure we were smiling. I hated all the fussing she did, but somehow the pictures always came out just right, so I guess it was worth it. My Dad, who was not a very patient man, would yell and curse at my Mom to hurry up but it didn't do any good, because my Mom was very persistent and would not allow my Dad to take the picture until everything was just right. As a result there are many pictures of me and my siblings with perfect posture, smiles, and our hair in place. I have to smile as I think about those times when my Mom was so obsessed with our perfection, but I also have to appreciate her as she just wanted her kids to look nice in the picture. This would make her feel proud when she showed the pictures to her friends or relatives. One day back in the 1960's my older brother brought home one of those Polaroid cameras that automatically printed the photos. My family thought it was really cool. It was like magic because one could watch the picture materialize before their eyes. When the image first appeared it was dark and kind of grizzly looking but eventually the shapes would take form and became the familiar pictures I still look at today. I think my Mom may have thrown away some of those Polaroid pictures that didn't quite materialize the way she expected them to. But that's OK because one could take numerous pictures since they didn't have to pay for the film processing. When I was older I got my own camera and I found my niche in life as I learned the art of

A picture of me with my brothers and sisters taken on a "picture perfect" Easter Sunday back in the 1960's.

picture taking. Now I was in control of the camera. I veered more towards the natural look so I liked to surprise my subjects and as a result I have many pictures that show my subject's real character. To this day I still prefer the "surprise" or "natural" shots. Unlike my parents who kept their pictures in the bottom drawer, I have a filing system for my pictures. I have a file which contains pictures of each of my children, my husband, my parents, my husband's parents and so on. It is one of my little obsessions to keep my pictures readily available and in order. On occasion my husband may find me in the closet where the file cabinet is kept, sitting on the floor gazing at my pictures. I have mentioned to my husband many times that if we ever have to evacuate due to a disaster that the pictures go with us. My husband and I have mentally rehearsed our evacuation plan and know which items we would take. I know my husband would not argue with me about taking the pictures because he knows how precious they are to me. The pictures are the essence of my life and the lives of those I cherish. When I think about my pictures I think of those hot sunny days in Arizona with my parents visiting my uncle. I think of that revolving aluminum Christmas tree my Dad loved so much. I think about my brothers and sisters as they laughed to themselves while Mom coached for us to stand still and smile. I think of my young children with their looks of innocence and surprise as they observed the world around them. I think of my Father and Mother as they got older and still displayed their affection for each other while I took their picture. I think of my grandchildren splashing around in the swimming pool on their floats, too young to have realized their dreams. I think of those family reunions with my Mom's family in Mississippi surrounded by old people and good food. I think of my handsome husband with his beard and tall figure. I think of the beautiful sunsets at the lake with the pine trees casting their shadows. I imagine that technology will continue to progress and as a result picture taking will change, but no matter how one takes a picture it will always be a reminder of our past. Because once the picture is taken it cannot be changed. One can argue about the past, but they cannot change it. I guess that's why a picture is so relevant, because it portrays a point in time that reminds us of who we were. So the next time you take a picture, remember you are preserving that moment in time and all the feelings and secrets associated with that few seconds the shutter opens to take the picture. Truly a picture is worth a thousand words, perhaps words that are hidden deep inside our souls. So smile and be happy with your life, because you never know when the camera will be shooting in your direction.

Living with Mr. Perfect

My husband is a very unique person in many ways. He is ten years younger than me but the age difference hasn't really affected our relationship, not yet anyways. My husband has that condition called "OTC" or is it 'CDS"? Well it's one of those three lettered syndromes that translates to obsessive tendencies, and that is putting it mildly. Anyways, he is very compulsive and sometimes it makes my life hell on earth. I am the victim of my husband's eccentricities which sometimes makes me feel like I am a prisoner in my own home. My husband has a philosophy of how he wants to live, and he expects me to act the part of his ongoing play in the stage of life. His philosophy is that everything has to be in order. And I became a player when I said "I do". Thank God I have a lot of patience which has helped our relationship to survive. I think I am able to cope with his condition because I really do care about my husband. Now I should have got a clue when I first met him, and he told me he washed his car "several times a week". But that one got passed me. Then we moved into our first house in 1994. There was carpet in the living room, just as there is in millions of homes across America. But one morning as I was getting ready for work and I heard the vacuum cleaner running. Now keep in mind it's around 4:00 am. I'm thinking "what the hell?" My husband later explained to me that it's a good idea to vacuum everyday. Well, as long as he's the one doing it, I guess I can accept that. And so he continued his "crack of dawn" vacuuming routine for the whole time we lived in that house. Now on the weekends it was my turn to vacuum, both upstairs and downstairs. But I didn't get off the hook that easy, as there was an art to vacuuming according to my husband and I would soon be his apprentice of that art. My husband explained to me that I had to vacuum backwards, so my footprints wouldn't be visible on the areas where I had already vacuumed. The first time he explained this to me I looked at him like he was a crazy man. Do you have any idea how hard it is to vacuum backwards? You have the cord behind you, which you constantly have to pick up and move so you don't trip over it. And there the obstacles behind you that you sometimes forget about, like the coffee table, the couch, the walls and so on. But I dutifully obeyed my husband's wishes because I know how fragile his condition is and I didn't want to annoy him. Thankfully we don't live in that house anymore, and our new house has tile floors in the living area, so there is no more early morning vacuuming. Of course my husband's condition has rendered many strange symptoms. I was asked nicely to put the dishtowels in the drawer facing a certain direction. If I failed to do this I would soon discover that they are corrected the next time I open the drawer. It's like the little CDS fairy flies around our house rearranging things so that everything is in its proper place. When things are not in their proper place my husband becomes very upset, like when he discovers the hand towels in our bathroom are facing the wrong direction. A few times I got confused and hung the towels facing the wrong direction. This made my husband more upset as he had to physically show me the correct way to hang the towels. Of course he yelled the whole time he was showing me which made the whole scene unpleasant. Now I don't know about most people, but at our house when one uses the bathroom or kitchen sink, they must wipe it out so it is dry. In other words after I was the dishes I must wipe the sink and faucet so it is dry and there are no spots on the faucet. Afterwards my husband will take a minute to inspect the faucet. If I miss a spot my husband will get a towel and wipe the spots off. It is very annoying because he is tall and can see behind the faucet but I am short and cannot. When I try to reason with my husband that I cannot see all the spots because I am not as tall, he just ignores me and continues to wipe off the couple of spots I missed. I finally concluded that you cannot reason with my husband when he is in one of his compulsive modes. This condition also affects our schedules, to which we cannot stray too far from. For instance every Saturday morning we clean the house. When I awaken there are three cups of brewed coffee waiting for me in the microwave. After I enjoy my first cup of coffee and a smoke, my husband begins his gazing at the clock routine until his patience runs out and he asks, "What time are we going to start cleaning?" I don't usually give him a good answer, so he announces we will start in fifteen minutes, and we usually do, rather I like it or not. God forbid if something out of the ordinary happened to upset our Saturday morning routine, such as a funeral or unexpected visit from a friend or family member, everything would be out of whack for my husband. He would become very anxious and stir crazy, like a wild animal. His condition also affects how he buys things, for instance he bought a new boat back in 2004. But that wasn't the end of it. He proceeded to buy replacement parts for the whole boat! I mean the whole boat! (Just in case something broke in the next twenty years or so). We have one bedroom full of boat parts which includes the seats, the radio, the steering wheel, the windshield, the cup holders and even the carpet. Did I mention the windshield? Oh yea, I did. One day I was kidding my husband and I told him he could build a new boat from all the spare parts he had in the bedroom. I thought it was funny, he did not. You see, people with this condition do not think rationally. Most people would buy a boat, and maybe a few spare parts, and when the boat was old they would simply replace it with a newer boat. So if you know someone with this condition, you have to learn how to compromise. And I believe there is good in every person, along with a few oddities. I myself display some characteristics that are not normal. Such as whenever I am folding clothes, filing papers at work or putting up dishes, I have to sort everything first. I have to make little stacks of the items I am putting up before I put them away. I am also strangely drawn to certain things when I go to the store, such as writing pens, cheap custom jewelry, greeting cards with glitter on them and fragrances. I spend an extra few minutes on the candle isle whenever I go grocery shopping. When no one is looking I pick up a few candles and relish the different fragrances. So you see, we all have our quirks. The important thing about being in a relationship is you have to look at the big picture. If you can get past the little annoyances and hang ups, and you see yourself as a happy person in the relationship, you probably made a good choice. Sometimes I like to tease my husband by upsetting his sock and underwear drawer. It just looks so perfect, all those white underwear, perfectly folded and stacked on top of each other. So when I put his socks in the drawer, I accidentally bump one of his perfects stacks of underwear so they appear to be the "leaning tower of underwear". It makes me so happy. Yes, it is a sick world we live in, but sometimes it is fun too.

Something for Everyone

I have a sister who is a few years older than me. She is a real character who is very out spoken. You just never know what she is going to say. She has worked hard all her life and now lives comfortably with her third husband. Now my sister was born in New Jersey, but you would never know it when she speaks with her Texas drawl. Of course she was transported to Texas by my parents at a very young age. She is a short person, barely five feet tall and well endowed for someone of her petite frame. She has a feisty, passionate personality. Don't cross her though, or you will be sorry. Deep down inside she is a caring, generous and beautiful person. Now I mention my sister because she loves to buy clothes. She has clothes in her closet that still have the tags attached because she has forgotten that she purchased them. Her clothes have filled the closets of her master bedroom and all the other bedrooms closets of her home. I could only imagine that if a burglar were to break into her house while she was at home, she would stand guard in front of her closet with a shotgun and wouldn't hesitate to shoot. Now I am not obsessed with clothes but I love music. I wish the air could be filled with music. There is something about music that makes me happy. I can be having the most miserable day and once I get into my car and turn on the radio I begin to feel redeemed as the stress from my day slowly disappears with each song. For every article of clothing my sister owns, I probably have a music CD, and my sister has a shit load of clothes. I think we all cling to something that brings us happiness in this messed up world, and somehow it transforms us. I guess you never really know a person till you know what their passion is. Now for some their passion is in their downfall. Some seek alcohol or drugs for their outlet. Others seek food or the roll of the dice. I guess there is a fine line between addiction and passion. To clarify though, I believe addiction is more like a necessity, or something one must have to survive, whereas passion is more like a fulfillment of something you want. Either way people seek it out. I don't know how it started, but my daughter started collecting frogs, not real frogs of course, but frog figurines. She finds them cute and interesting to look at. My husband likes to collect WWII memorabilia. Even with his humble earnings he has managed to acquire quite a collection of stuff. My husband is also obsessed with the History Channel and loves to watch programs related to World War II. He can identify any gun, ship, tank or plane from that era. I think he was reincarnated from that age. Well, whatever your passion is, you are entitled to it if it gives you peace of mind, a warm fuzzy feeling inside or takes your mind off this troublesome world. So I say to all you collectors and would be collectors, know your limitations. Don't let your passion interfere with your responsibilities in life, or you will let someone down. And one day when you meet that special person in your life, check out their surroundings. It may tell you something about that person you never knew.

All that Glitters

I recently received an entry to enter a contest to win a diamond watch. I had to write a small paragraph about why I wanted to win the diamond watch which contained thirty five words or less. I managed to do so and sealed my fate as I put the sweepstakes entry in the mailbox. I already knew I wouldn't win, but the lure of that diamond watch was too irresistible. Besides us girls will do anything, well almost anything, for diamonds. For the sweepstakes entry I wrote "I like diamonds, I like diamonds, I like diamonds, I like diamonds, I like diamonds, I like diamonds, I like diamonds, I really like diamonds, I really like diamonds, I really like diamonds, I love diamonds". Whoops, that's thirty six words. I know it was silly to write that as an afterthought. I remember when my first husband got me a promise ring back when I was only seventeen years old. I thought it was true love that inspired him, but the diamond was so small in that ring that I should have gauged our relationship on it. I was young and perhaps the fogginess of what I thought was true love clouded my perception. During my marriage to my first husband I thought he might like to replace that insignificant diamond with something more worthy, but four children and fourteen years of marriage never resulted in another diamond. So I proceeded to marry my second husband. Our wedding bands were simple and did not contain the diamond I was hoping for. What is the deal, is it a trend? I mean I have given my second husband so many hints which have yet to yield that little black box. Now I'm not expecting a diamond on the "Elizabeth Taylor" scale, just a simple one or two karat diamond would do. A couple of years ago my children presented me with a "mother's ring" which contained by children's birthstones. One of the birthstones is a diamond because one of my children has a birthday in the month of April. And while it is not a large diamond, I will treasure it forever as it is set in the ring next to the birthstones of my other children. Now here are some words of advice for you men out there, if you really care about your partner, give them a diamond at least once. It is best to surprise them in a romantic setting. And you know diamonds are not just for women. I don't understand why women can't give their male partner's a diamond? I hate the commercials on TV that always show men giving diamonds to women. I think they should make a commercial that shows a woman presenting diamond jewelry to her man. What about a gay person presenting diamond jewelry to their gay partner? After all, the world has changed along with our portrayal of relationships. I think the jewelry companies need to be more up to date on modern relationships and reflect it in their advertising. Well, the days are getting shorter now as I am in the late afternoon of my life. I might just have to settle for the ocean cruise my husband and I have been discussing for the last decade or so. Or maybe I will just go to the jewelry store one day and buy a beautiful, expensive piece of diamond jewelry for myself and wear it with a look of revenge when I surprise my husband. No I don't think that is my character, so I will just continue gazing at all those heavenly diamonds in the night sky and dropping the occasional hint to my husband. But I will definitely have a talk with my sons about this, because I don't want the woman of their dreams to have to wait for the inevitable diamond. And for all you more fortunate women out there who have been bestowed with diamonds, I hope the man in your life is worthy of the diamonds you flaunt. In the meantime I'll keep my sunglasses handy in case I get one of those real sparklers.

Christmas Lane

Ever since I was a young girl I have loved Christmas time. It is that time of year when humanity seems to be transformed as people become caring and thoughtful for a season. Back in the early 1960's my parents bought one of those revolving aluminum Christmas trees that was accompanied by a color wheel that would shine different colors on it while it revolved. It was so beautiful. As a young child I would lie on the couch and watch it endlessly until I drifted off to sleep. I suppose my mother or father would awaken me or carry me off to my bed afterwards. I have so many wonderful memories of Christmas time with my family who made it a joyous occasion. I was the next to the youngest in our family. I had an older brother, three older sisters and a younger brother. My father worked hard to support our family while my mother stayed home and took care of us kids. I learned at an early age that the Thanksgiving holiday was the prelude to the Christmas season and the excitement started as soon as we finished our Thanksgiving dinner complete with turkey soup, (one of my mom's specialties), turkey and dressing and homemade pie. December was just around the corner which brought my birthday and Christmas. Needless to say December was a very

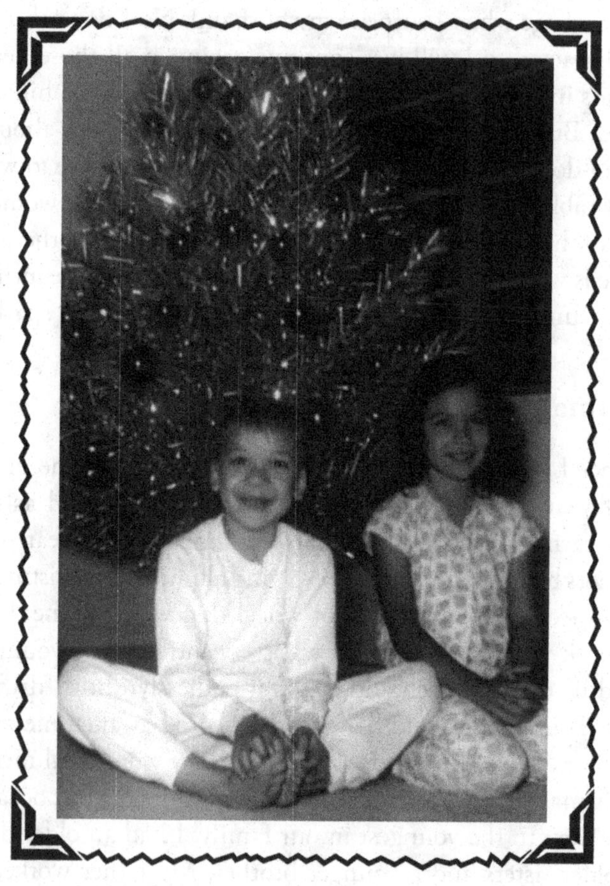

My brother and I sitting next to our "retro" aluminum Christmas tree.

exciting time for me as a young girl. I would be bestowed with gifts for my birthday and Christmas. But it was much more than gifts that made me love the season. It was the thoughtfulness that went into buying the gifts, the gift wrapping my mother would try to make so complete, my father's mood which was happy and childlike, the discussions of where to put the ornaments on the Christmas tree, the fruit bowl my mother would remove from the cabinet to fill with fruit and nuts, the visit to see Santa Claus who would take time out of his busy schedule to ask me what I wanted for Christmas, the windows I would stare out which felt cold and wet from the December rains, the fallen leaves in the yard, the smell of wood burning in the fireplace and I could go on and on to describe all the wonderful memories. I especially liked all the glitter and gleam of Christmas time. The shiny ribbons that decorated the gifts, the tinsel that wrapped around the Christmas tree, the lights my dad hung outside on the roof, the foil decoration that covered the front door and the shiny ornaments that hung from the tree, glistening in the light as they moved slightly from time to time.

It was all so magical. Now I am older but the memories of Christmas time have not faded. I am blessed that I am able to share some of those memories with my children who are now grown up. Now here's a twist to all the wonder and splendor I just portrayed. I have a recurring dream that it is the day before Christmas and I have not decorated the house or bought any Christmas presents. In my dream I am in a mad rush to get to the store the night before Christmas and buy some presents. The stores are filled with people and I begin to panic as I realize I may not be able to finish my Christmas shopping in time. Afterwards in my dream it is either Christmas Eve or Christmas morning and I scurry to find a few decorations up in the attic so I can decorate before my company arrives. I don't know why but I dream this dream over and over, all throughout the year. As my own dream analyst I suppose it means I need to be more organized and make better preparations. How ironic it is that the time I love most in my life becomes a nightmare in my dreams. Maybe I am just confused. Whatever the reason for my recurring nightmare I will continue to love Christmas time as long as I am able to remember what it means to me. I have a Christmas wish of building a house on a lone street and my family would build their own houses on the same street. I would name the street "Christmas Lane" and I could visit my family everyday. At Christmas time the whole street would be decorated on a huge scale and everyone would take a two week vacation from their jobs. We would go shopping together, bake pies and cakes, wrap presents and play my father's old Christmas albums on the record player. We would watch old Christmas movies and have a wonderful time. Now I know this is just a dream and it will never happen but Christmas time is a time of dreams. So I will continue to love Christmas time and all it represents. I will not forget the true meaning of Christmas which is the birth of Jesus and that's what it's really all about. Jesus changed our world forever and his birth meant salvation for those who accept him. If we as humankind could bestow the joy, kindness and generosity of Christmas time throughout the year this world would be a much better place to live in. And I believe the heavens and earth would truly have a reason to celebrate. What a concept.

Human Nature

We humans are a very strange species indeed. We have evolved for generations and become quite civilized and intellectual through the years. But are we really civilized? Perhaps we are civilized because we have to be to exist in today's modern world. But if society was to break down, our true nature, our primeval core would resurface again. So maybe there are a mixture of many things that make us each unique, society, the way we were raised, our education and our desires and logic. Because let's face it, we are emotional beings, and that's what makes us good, bad or something in between.

Peace from Within, that's All We Need

As I mentioned we humans are a strange species. We are composed of many emotions that make us unique individuals based on our upbringing and social backgrounds. Some of us are kind, giving and loving, while others are hateful and deceitful. I believe we all have the ability to change, but most people do not change drastically. Most of us exhibit a combination of traits, both good and bad as part of our personality. For example I was raised in a large family and learned that sharing and giving was important. My husband on the other hand was raised as an only child. While he can be giving, he is more self centered than I am. I think a person must be secure with their inner feelings to find peace. If one was to write down the things they like and dislike about their selves, they might be surprised at what they see written on paper. So I challenge anyone to do this, and I will start by writing my own list. I have chosen three traits I do not like about myself, so the challenge is on. Number one, I am impatient. I hate to wait in line at the grocery store, the bank or basically anywhere. To me waiting is just a waste of time. However one place I don't mind waiting is when I'm in line at the amusement park to get on one of those thrill rides. I become anxious when I know it is my turn to get on the ride. My heart begins to beat faster, my palms feel sweaty and the faint smile I display is just a veil to hide my fear of getting on the ride. I observe the other people and notice the ones towards the end of the line seem happy and excited. But as the crowd pushes towards the front of the line, there is a predictable silence. It is the silence of anticipation, knowing that you are going to risk your life for a ten minute ride that once you commit to, there is no way to exit. That feeling of doom overwhelms me as the ride starts, they lock me down so to speak and I have only seconds to change my mind. However I don't want to be a sissy so I stay seated, waiting for the inevitable thrill that is going to scare the crap out of me. It seems everyone else on the ride is oblivious to my fear, or perhaps they are enveloped in their own fear? As the ride begins I hear the metal clanking in rhythm. One knows that when that sound subsides the exhilaration begins, carrying us off to a new thrill which are bodies were not intended for. Somehow I survive the ride and exit with a sense of accomplishment. Anyways, I do consider myself to be impatient. Maybe it stems from my younger years when I lived in a small house with my Father, Mother and five brothers and sisters. There was only one bathroom for us to share, yes I believe that is what started it. And I feel as though I have been waiting all my life. Waiting for the clerk in the grocery store to stop making small talk and get me checked out so I get on with my life, waiting for the car in front of me at the drive-thru bank, while the customer inside the car discusses all their banking discrepancies, waiting for my neighbor to stop talking about dumb shit so I can go inside and watch television. Waiting for Jesus to come back and save the world from all the corruption and violence, but somehow I don't think he will come back while I'm still alive. Now I have revealed my first bad trait so let's move on. The number two trait I don't like about myself is that I am gullible. By being gullible anyone can usually talk me into anything. This is not good. I have gotten into some pretty sticky situations by being gullible. My Mother always taught me to go with my first instinct. I know I should have listened to her. When I was younger my so called friends could talk me into anything because I was afraid to say no. I am probably a smoker today because when I was offered a cigarette back in my school days and I didn't know how to say "no" and that mistake started a lifetime of smoking cigarettes. And it got worse as I was afraid to say no to other substances which I will not name in this chapter as I do not want to incriminate myself. Later in life my gullibility became evident as I was afraid to say "no" to total strangers asking for money, or those sly magazine salespeople who stood at my door front. Yes it's really hard being "Mrs. Nice Guy" all your life. Now on to the third trait I don't like about myself which is my lack of self confidence. If you met me at a party, you would have to be the one to initiate a conversation because I probably wouldn't. Rather you would probably find me behind the scenes sitting at a table quietly sipping on a drink. I think people who are self confident carry themselves differently. They walk and talk with an air of confidence. Maybe they have better posture or hold their heads up higher. They are not embarrassed easily and they know how to talk to other people. As I reflect back on my younger years I think I understand why I am not a confident person. I had three older sisters who should have been my mentors by teaching me how to dress for success and do all those other sisterly things when I was younger. The problem was my sisters were six to nine years older than me. When I finally reached the age where I needed their guidance, they all abandoned ship and got married. So during my formative teen years I didn't have anyone to teach me all the social skills I would need later in life. As a result I succumbed to being a loner if you will. Sure I had a few friends, friends who were also loners like me. I had no direction in my young life so I spent hours in my room listening to records and admiring my black light posters while I wrote poetry. I am still lacking in confidence but most people who meet me just think I am a quite person. So I just go with the flow. Now if you took the three traits I mentioned about myself, impatient, gullible and lacking self confidence and I have a surprise for everyone. To prove that a trait does not make one a good or bad person, let me reveal how those traits can be positive. Impatience could be translated as ambitious, gullibility could be translated as generous, and lacking self confidence could be translated as gentle or easy going. It is how one perceives these traits that make them what they are. It is important that every person realize they are unique and appreciate their self worth. I think part of the problem is how people label other people. I think those people are just ignorant. So the next time you stand in front of the mirror, try to focus on the inner you. Are you a caring person? Do you help other people? Are you a strong person? Are you creative? Are you a good parent? You see one person can be many things and it is up to the next person to find the goodness in that person. So smile and try to find the peace within despite your so called "negative traits". After all we're only human

Disconnected

You probably won't believe this, but I do not own a cell phone. I know it's amazing that I've survived without a cell phone thus far. I've purchased cell phones for my deserving children for whatever the occasion was. And I often paid their monthly phone bill for a couple of years or until they were able to take over the payments. I try to be a good mom. Plus I knew if my children had a phone during those vulnerable years I could get in touch with them at almost anytime, so I had a good reason for being so generous. But for real, I don't know how I have survived without a cell phone this long. Everywhere I go people are talking on their cell phones, in their cars as they veer over into my lane while I'm driving down the road, in the grocery store, at the gas station, even the public bathrooms. It is a frenzy that won't go away. I've even seen cell phones for toddlers, which is totally ridiculous. But why do I need a cell phone? I guess it would be convenient to have a cell phone in case I got lost while I was driving and I could call someone for directions. Or if I was late for an occasion I could call my party to let them know I was running late. I could call my husband while I'm doing my Saturday errands to see if I need to stop at the liquor store. I could also call my husband when he goes to the home improvement store on Saturday morning and tell him to pick me up a pack of cigarettes. It sure would be cool if people would have their cell phone numbers on their license plates, then you could call them up while you were driving and say "Hey jerk, where did you learn to drive?", or something to that effect. Of course the driver you were calling would never be able to figure who called them because practically everyone driving would be talking on their cell phones. I remember back in the seventies and eighties, the only distraction people had when they were driving was when the looked down to change the radio station, or maybe they had to light their cigarette and had to look down to push in the lighter that most cars had available. Now it's like another world, every driver has one hand on the steering wheel, and one hand holding their cell phone. If they smoke or have to hold a drink they are probably driving with no hands. At first when cell phones were introduced into our naïve society, they were expensive and used mostly by professionals. They were called mobile phones and people would use the phone for a quick conversation or in case of an emergency as the phone companies usually charged by the minute for their use. Now the phone companies have become wiser and offer phone plans that include millions of minutes, (yes I am being sarcastic), free long distance, text messaging, voicemail, free nights and weekends, and shared plans for callers who are on the same plan. People have become addicted to using their cell phones constantly. They search out for people to call as they scroll down their list of phone numbers to seek out their next victim. It has become obscene. I've even seen co-workers who will be talking to a customer on the phone at work, and having a conversation on their cell phone at the same time. I sometimes carpool with my husband and it is not unusual for us to leave the house as early as 4:30 am. Sometimes while my husband is driving we'll pass a car and the person driving will be talking on their cell phone. My husband and I look at each other and wonder who in the hell would they be talking to so early in the morning? When I wake up in the morning, I really don't feel like talking to anyone. I just want to enjoy the peace and quite. And besides, I couldn't think of anyone to call early in the morning. I don't really have any friends, and if I called my family members, they would think something was wrong. One day I will probably get a cell phone so I can be like everyone else. Now what about phone etiquette? For those of you that do own a cell phone you should never talk on your cell phone when you are with a live person. It is very rude. If your phone rings, and you must answer it, tell the caller you will call them back. Secondly, it is rude to talk on the phone while you are doing a business transaction, such as paying for something at the grocery store or doing your banking. If the clerk needs to ask you something, they feel awkward about interrupting you. So for God's sake, just put your phone down for a couple of fucking minutes! And here's one more, if you go to a family outing, it is rude if you spend the whole time talking on your cell phone or text messaging. Can't you socialize with your family for a short time? You might always have a phone but Grandpa isn't going to live forever. Remember, there are things that are more important than the phone numbers you have stored in your phone. And for Heaven sakes please turn down the volume on your stupid ring tones when you step away from your phone. It's just using good manners. If you're not going to answer the phone put it on vibrate or something. I wish for one day, no let's say one week, that all the satellites in space would stop functioning. Maybe a CME from space would knock them out. Oh, CME stands for "corolla mass ejection". I read about it in a magazine article one day while I was in a waiting room. Of course reading while one is a waiting room is probably a thing of the past as nowadays most people are playing with their phones instead. I guess I am one of the few people who read to pass the time. Now back to the article I was discussing. CME is an event where the sun ejects flares far into space which can affect our space satellites and cause all kinds of havoc. Anyways, it would be pretty cool if one of those sun flares would just swipe by earth enough to temporarily cause the satellites to dysfunction for say a few days, just a baby solar flare perhaps. People would be starring at their cell phones in disbelief, pushing the buttons randomly in a desperate attempt to make them work. They would walk around like wind up people bumping into each other because their eyes would be focused downward on their phones. They would drive to the nearest store to buy batteries and phone chargers only to discover that nothing they did would make their phones work. But wait, they may not be able to drive to the store because the solar flares could stop cars engines from working similar to an EMP effect. (Electro magnetic pulse).It would be mass hysteria. All the while the phone companies would be thinking about how much money they were going to loose and how they were going to handle the crisis. I could see people rushing to payphones to call someone. I think the last time I used a payphone it was .50 cents, but it would only work if you had the correct change, or do payphones take credit and debit cards now? Oh this is too amusing because I would be laughing, laughing as society became disconnected. And I would enjoy every priceless, silent minute while it lasted. O.K., maybe I am a little disconnected from reality, but that's what makes life interesting sometimes.

Ageing Sucks

Oh, the golden years that people talk about. That leisurely time one spends between retirement and death. That time when one can reflect on their life on this earth and hopefully produce a smile or two. I am not looking forward to it at all! My older brother who just turned sixty five recently retired. Fortunately he is still in good health and good spirits. He spends his days doing yard work, making trips to the store and cooking dinner as he has always enjoyed cooking. What scares me though is that I am still quite a bit younger than my older brother, but as you grow up observing your siblings you soon realize a pattern. That pattern is that whatever happens to them in the ageing process will happen to me next. For instance when I was a young girl with dreams of being independent, one of my three older sisters got married. It was an exciting time and she soon moved into an apartment with her new husband. I was still in my teenage years and perhaps I was a little bit jealous of my sister's new life. I still had to go to school and do homework, obey my parents and tolerate my younger brother's teasing and harassments. All this while my older sister was free to go shopping whenever she wished, drive her car wherever she wanted to go and stay up as late as she wanted to. At that time in my life I thought I would never reach the age of twenty one, much less eighteen. That seemed an eternity away. Well, I did reach eighteen and was married before I turned nineteen. By the age of twenty seven I had brought four wonderful children into the world. By the age of thirty four I was divorced and married again. Now here I am at a somewhat stagnant time in my life that is somewhere between youth and death, wondering where all the time went. It seems the sunsets come a lot quicker these days as I prepare for bedtime after a long day of work at the office. I don't like bedtime because it is too quite. After I get in bed I have to adjust my body to a comfortable sleeping position which is not easy with all the aches and pains I experience. Finally I get comfortable but I can't seem to fall asleep. I stare out the window or at the ceiling as my mind becomes a race track for all the thoughts I have stored during my lifetime. I wonder what my children are doing, well they're not really children anymore, and that's the part that bothers me. When my children were young I had control of their lives. Now they are in control of their own lives. I continue to lie in the bed and discover a new pain I didn't have before. I begin to self diagnose my aches and pains while I lay there in the bed. At my age it any ache or pain could be serious or even life threatening. Then the pain goes away and I forget about it. My mind wonders again as I think about my unborn grandchild, what will he or she look like? I think about my younger sons who have not married yet. What is taking them so long to get settled into life? Finally I began to drift asleep and another day slips away. The problem is that too many days have slipped away. I am trying desperately to hold on to my middle ages, but the signs are there. The signs of ageing that is, which are starting to appear on a daily basis. Such as I notice my hearing is not as good as it used to be. My gray hair seems to present itself more often these days, which means more trips to the hair salon. My body has reacted as well. I never was the super model type, but I had always managed my weight pretty good. Now I have bulges where I didn't have bulges before. Where the hell did they come from? I haven't really changed my diet, but it seems these bulges just appeared one morning after I got out of the shower and noticed them in the mirror as I was drying off. Now I understand why my mother used to wear those pants with the elastic waistbands. Thankfully I have not had to succumb to bifocal eyeglasses yet, but I know it's just a matter of time. And what about those hot flashes? There's no way to describe them except for a few seconds it feels like your body is under attack by one of those secret military ray guns. The hot flashes come without warning and no matter how discreet you are they are worthy a few choice words such as "what the hell?" And with all these problems I am facing I have to deal with a husband who is ten years younger than me. Translation, I have to appear and act younger than I am. This is not an easy task. It means that I have to age under the radar so to speak. I can't complain about all my aches and pains too much because that would be a bad sign to my husband. But I do have a battle plan, which is to save up enough money to get plastic surgery. One day I will come home and look twenty years younger, maybe I will even look younger than my husband? Imagine that, a thirty year old face on a middle aged body? I suppose I will have to start exercising so when that fateful day to the plastic surgeon does arrive I will be in good shape. Hopefully I will be able to save up the money before it is too late. Speaking of money, that is another issue of ageing. I am starting to think about my retirement and wondering where the retirement money is going to come from. I have a decent paying job but I don't really make enough money to stash away for those golden years. The price of gasoline, food, taxes and everything else keeps spiraling up while my wages stay about the same. I just hope my children won't mind if I have to move in with them one day. Last but not least I wonder about the finality of my life. Where does one go after they die? I can only hope that I have been a good person and that God will find me worthy. Now I am starting to understand why the churches of America are filled with old people. After one has lived much of their life, they began to ponder where they will spend eternity, so they flock to the churches to ensure their salvation. I believe younger people are just too busy raising their families and pursuing their careers, therefore church and going to heaven is not too high on their list of priorities. Perhaps it should be though, just in case one never reaches old age, as there are no guarantees of tomorrow. I imagine the worst fear I have of ageing is loosing my memory. I noticed I forget things more easily, such as where I parked the car. As I walk outside to the store parking lot I fumble for my sunglasses, then I stop for a moment to remember where I parked. I didn't do this when I was younger. Sometimes I can only remember the general area where I parked, so I proceed in that direction, then I become panicked, only to notice my car was parked a couple of rows away. I make a sharp turn and wonder if anyone noticed my confusion. Well at my age I don't really care what anyone thinks so I hold my head up high and walk towards the car. Of course this doesn't happen every time I park; but it is starting to happen more often than I like. Mostly I think it is the unknown things about ageing that disturb me. But I guess I will just have to wait and see what happens. In the meantime I'll be keeping tabs on my siblings to see how they age. Maybe if they can handle it so can I, besides I don't really have a choice, time will eventually be victorious.

My Purse

You real men out there may want to skip this chapter as it relates to women and their purses. Most women carry a purse because we have to. But a purse is not just a container to carry our personal possessions in. A purse is more than shaped leather or vinyl. Rather a purse is a representation of a woman and her existence in the world. Some women prefer to carry a purse overstuffed and overflowing with all the necessities of her busy life. Other woman prefer to carry a large suitcase like purse which stores more possessions than she really needs, but is comforting like a child's security blanket. Other women are more concerned with the purse than the contents and prefer to carry designer bags which give them status and splendor as they extract their collection of credit cards to pay at the store counter. I prefer to carry a large purse, but for practical reasons. I have many important things that must be present with me in order to maintain my sanity in this disorderly life of mine. Most important is my daily planner. Well, it used to be a daily planner until I dissected it by tearing out all the calendar pages so I could use the leather binder for its many compartments it had to offer. I use the compartments to stash my important papers and organize my bills and such. I also use the planner to hold my one and only credit card, directions to the dog breeder's house in case my husband and I decide to get a dog, some pretty rose stickers that I forget I had, postage stamps, my bank account register and miscellaneous mail I didn't have time to read. There is no way in hell all this stuff could fit into a man's wallet, which is why women carry purses. If you go deeper into my purse you will find my small cosmetic bag. It is the essence of life to many women who would not be caught dead without their make up. Now I don't like to wear too much make up but I do carry the bare necessities. I have several tubes of lipstick which range from the type that plumps your lips to make them look fuller, to the type that is suppose to last all day regardless of how many cups of coffee I drink. I also carry eye shadow to define my eyes and detract would be lookers from the creases and lines I display when I express myself. Most important is the small mirror that I very seldom use but I can retrieve in case of an emergency and I need to spot check my appearance. The mirror is small so I can only check a certain portion of my face at one time. I usually check my nose to make sure it is not shiny, or my lips to make sure my lipstick hasn't worn off. Of course I have very few emergency encounters where my compact mirror is needed. I can remember my mother though, who would predictably pull out her compact mirror at the end of our family road trips to check her appearance. She would hastily apply lipstick as my dad drove to the end of our destination. The friends or relatives we were visiting never knew about my mom's last minute lipstick and powder applications, I'm sure they were just glad to see her and thought she looked beautiful. My dad would sometimes make commentaries about my mom's last minute make up applications. I can't remember his exact words, but the commentaries usually made my mom mad and she would utter a few retaliatory words, and the whole scene would make us kids chuckle in the backseat. Now back to the contents of my purse, but I have to admit I do enjoy the daydreaming. The rest of the contents of my purse are pretty simple. My keys, which allow me to have access to my car, my house, my office and few more keys that would allow me entry to somewhere else but I can't remember where. My prescription eyeglasses I wear when I'm driving at night or in the rain, my prescription sunglasses that I wear when I'm driving and it's sunny outside, my driver's license, a little bit of cash, some coins leftover from purchases I made and which haven't made it to the coin jar yet. Of course since I'm a smoker I have to carry a pack of cigarettes and sometimes two packs if one pack is almost empty. I also carry two cigarette lighters because I inevitably leave one at work on the conversation table as I make small talk with my co-workers. Now occasionally a stray item appears in my purse as the situation may necessitate its existence. These items may include a camera for family gatherings, vacations and such. Sometimes I carry gift wrapping supplies such as ribbon, scissors and greeting cards in my purse for those occasions when I must wrap gifts in the car. Of course I usually forget the tape and after I curse at my husband for making me leave on time, I somehow manage to be creative enough with the ribbon as not to require the tape after all. Sometimes I carry medicine in my purse if I have to go somewhere and I'm not feeling well. Now I have a suggestion for all you women out there carrying your purses of choice, regardless of the contents. First of all never carry your social security card in your purse or wallet. You should have the number memorized and there's no need to carry it. If anyone should steal your purse and find your social security card they could steal your identity. Another tip, please don't leave your purse in the shopping cart unattended. It is easy for someone to grab your wallet or purse as you step away from the cart. One more thing, please have easy access to your money, credit or debit cards or whatever the hell you use to pay with at the store counter. There is nothing more frustrating than standing in line behind some dumb ass woman who can't find her checkbook, her credit card or cash. So instead of reading those trashy magazines at the counter here's a plan, you women out there should use those precious few minutes to locate your method of payment before you check out! I have to admit that men do not have this problem; they are always ready to check out with cash or credit card in hand before the total is given. I guess I am a cashier's dream come true also. When I check out at the store I watch the register as my items are tallied so I can almost predict what the total will be. As soon as the cashier announces the total I hand over the cash. Let's face it, my time is precious and I have more important things to do than organize my purse at the check out counter. Often times while I am in line to check out I observe women and their purses. You may wonder what a purse tells about the woman who carries it. Well here are some thoughts on that subject. A purse that is overflowing and disorganized would tell me that the owner is disorganized or has too many things going on in her life. That's not necessarily a bad thing, if she has a lot going on she may be surrounded by family and friends who keep her busy in a positive way. She may enjoy the hectic closeness of all those around her. A small purse lacking of contents would tell me the owner is afraid to venture out in life and may be lacking in confidence. The woman who carries a small purse may need more of everything if you will, including love and friendship. A purse that is worn or broken tells me that the owner is either too poor to replace the purse or has no self esteem. For many years I could only afford one purse at a time. I had to purchase it carefully because I would be stuck with it until I could afford to buy another one. My purses were always neutral colors such as brown or black because it had to match whatever I was wearing. But I have to confess that I always wanted a shiny, red purse. I was inspired as a young girl one day when my mom and a good friend of hers were getting ready to go out to dinner. Her lady friend pulled out a shiny red purse with matching shoes as the two of them dressed for dinner. My eyes were glued to that red purse because I had never seen my mom with a shiny red purse. My mom was too conservative to wear a shiny red purse. Ever since that memorable day I think of that red purse and one day I will march into my favorite store and buy a red purse and no one will be able to stop me. I don't know what a red purse would tell about a woman, I imagine it would be something intriguing though. When I do find that red purse I have been dreaming of for decades I will wear it proudly and inside that purse will be a little bit of magic as the memories of my childhood will be with me whenever I carry it. For now I will have to be satisfied with the purse I have. It is an oversized purse which is a shiny platinum color. It has extra compartments for carrying a cell phone or keys. Since I don't have a cell phone I use the cell phone compartment to carry my cigarettes. I also like the platinum color because it matches almost everything I wear. So ladies just remember, the next time you are out and about, someone might be observing you and your purse. So wear it proudly no matter the color or the style, and keep it close to you, because your purse is like your life in a little bag. What you put into that bag, is what you get out of it, so choose the contents wisely.

Perception

I have to admit that writing this book has been a challenge. I don't think society will change overnight or that anyone will really consider the changes I have written about, but at least the word is out. If I am able to make a positive influence on the powers to be, then I have accomplished what I set out to do. I have so many ideas but so little time as we are only on this earth for a season. I wonder, does God look down upon us and wonder about His creation? Or is God fed up with us and our destructive nature? We humans are supposed to live in harmony with nature and creation as a whole. I would have to say that a small minority of humankind actually do live in harmony with nature. The rest of us are just trying to survive and pay the bills. Just remember though that everything you do today or tomorrow will be history next week. We are living our own legacy everyday and the sum of what we do is in effect how we will be remembered. Here's a thought. We judge others many times by the way they are dressed or how they look to us. I'm talking about strangers of course and sense one doesn't know that person who is a stranger the only way we can judge them is by appearance. But appearance is more than the

My children when they were young. They are the most precious assets I have. They filled my heart with joy, laughter and love and they made me smile.

My children all grown up now and still making me smile. (It's amazing what a difference a few years can make).

clothes one wears or the way a person carries their self. Appearance can also be projected by the way a person acts. For instance a person could be dressed to perfection, but present an angry disposition and then that person is perceived as ugly or not worthy of our attention. On the other hand a person could be dressed poorly but carry their self in a confident manner with a smile and that person would be perceived as worthy of our attention. Many times I have noticed my husband looking at the back of a woman who appears to be attractive. Her body is toned and shapely and perhaps she has an appealing walk. Once my husband passes the woman his curiosity gives in and he turns to see her face. Surprisingly she may not be attractive in the face, so my husband continues his fast pace and probably wonders why he had noticed the woman. Well it just proves that no one is perfect. That same woman my husband passed could be someone's daughter, or perhaps someone's wife, or sister. So that same woman could be perceived as beautiful to her family or husband. You may wonder, what is my point? Well I just believe we need to be more objective and less subjective of our fellow humans. We as humans need to get along with each other because we're stuck on this rock hurling through space and there's nothing we can do about it. We don't need to invent more weapons of mass destruction which will sit in storage until we can figure out how and when to use them. Rather we need more philosophers and scientist to help us improve the quality of life. I believe humankind is misdirecting its energy in all the wrong places. Take the churches for instance. I see churches in the Houston area advertise on television on a regular basis. It takes money for all that advertising which I'm sure the church congregation gladly provides. Now if a church took all that money they paid for advertising and helped the homeless people on the streets, I feel that would be something positive. Speaking of homeless people, I think that is one of the most pathetic situations I've ever seen. How did these people become homeless? I don't think they were born that way. Many of those unfortunate souls were the victims of substance abuse, abusive parenting or just bad luck. Why doesn't the government provide housing and treatment for them? The homeless people may need an occasional free meal or warm blanket but what they really need is medical and mental health treatment. Why doesn't our medical society help these people? I see doctors who flock to other countries to provide free services to the poor who cannot afford medical care, but what about the homeless who walk the streets of their hometowns in America? The same principle applies to drug addicts who are arrested and put in jail. These addicts don't need to spend time in a jail rather they need treatment in a drug recovery program. I know we cannot solve all these problems, but maybe we just need to refocus our thought processes. For instance I know that every weekend I will clean my house. I would rather do something more enjoyable but I cannot afford a maid service. So I play music while I'm cleaning the house and somehow that dreaded chore becomes almost enjoyable as the music plays and I sing along while I'm scrubbing the toilet. You see without the music I would just be scrubbing the toilet. So maybe the important thing is not what we do, but how we choose to do it. Maybe we need to stop and talk to our neighbors instead of complaining about them. Maybe we need more backyard picnics. When my children were small they used to get restless when it would rain. Naturally children want to play outside. So I had an idea which was to have an inside picnic. I would make their lunch and spread it out on a blanket or sheet and we had our picnic in the house. The children loved it and it calmed their spirits for awhile. They even requested the inside picnic again when it would begin to rain. You see there are solutions if one tries to be imaginative enough to find them. We are blessed with the intelligence so all we need to do is apply to the right cause. And what is the right cause one might ask? The right cause is whatever it needs to be for that time and place in one's life. All we have to do is look around and notice the world before it is too late.

Summary

Well sometimes the last words are the hardest words to write. I would like to share a little bit about my family. Unfortunately my father and mother passed away when I was only thirty seven years old. This was hard to accept but I still see them in my dreams. I would like to believe that when I dream about them they are really there somehow, maybe in a spiritual realm of existence. I guess no matter how old I am I will always miss my father and mother. I have four children and I couldn't imagine my life without them. My firstborn son is a family man with a career in the military. He is very intelligent so don't get into an intellectual discussion with him because he will always prevail. He is also very committed to his family and career. He is a good father and husband and I am very proud of what he has accomplished. He has also been blessed with five wonderful children. My second born is my one and only daughter. She has chosen to be a teacher and is just starting her career. She is a loving and kind person. We are very close, almost like best friends as we confide in each other about all aspects of our lives. She is a new mother and I'm glad that she has experienced motherhood as it is one of the best experiences of life. I know in my heart that she will be successful in whatever endeavors she chooses as she is a very dedicated person. My third born is another son who is trying to find his direction in life. He was recently married and I hope his wittiness

A picture of my Father and Mother taken on the shores of Galveston, Texas during the 1950's.

and sense of humor will make him a compatible and loving husband. He is unpredictable so you never know what to expect when you're around him. He is warm, thoughtful and has a heart of gold. And his sense of humor always surprises me. My fourth born is another son who is also trying to find his niche in life but I feel he does not recognize his full potential. He is fun loving and sweet. He also loves children and animals so perhaps one of these days he will have a houseful of children or animals or perhaps both. I can also see the philosophical side of him as he always amazes me when we are talking. I believe he can accomplish many things once he becomes focused, so I can't wait to see how his life will evolve. I also have sisters and brothers who I don't get to see as often as I like. When my father and mother were alive the family was much closer as my parents were the center of our little universe. Now my sisters, brothers and I are like wandering sheep waiting for someone to herd us together. On occasions we do get together and enjoy reminiscing about the past.

I am married to my second husband and we really compliment each other. I believe we are truly soul mates. He is my rock, and sometimes my downfall. We have managed to stay together for almost twenty years so I think there's a possibility he will hang around till the end. Only time will tell.

You may wonder about me, the writer, what am I like? I am very quite, but not shy. I am caring but I don't always have the time or means to share with others. I am a little crazy and wild, but self disciplined. I am spontaneous, but careful. Last but not least, I am a dreamer. I dream of a perfect world and a perfect existence. But there are clouds on my horizon of the perfect world, and this plays with my head all the time. I get frustrated about things I cannot change. I guess I am not too different from most humans, as we all have our limitations. I feel that if I had more time I could make a difference, but time is what I don't have. If one could visualize their life when they are young and do all the right things, there would still not be enough time to accomplish everything. So I would have to say that time is the most precious resource we have as humans. Time should be used wisely, not foolishly. We are all born into the light, and fade into the darkness. It is that span between the light and the darkness that we call life. So live life to its fullest, before it fades away. I plan to do so to the best of my ability.

I would like to dedicate this book to my father and mother. I believe they are with me in spirit and always will be. They taught me how to live and laugh, how to work hard and enjoy life, how to be honest and sincere. I hope I can share these tributes with everyone I meet, and maybe they will understand where I came from.

The End